W9-BAF-823

JUST FOR
THE FRILL
OF IT

25 Flirty, Fabulous Styles to Make with Clothes You Already Own

JUST FOR THE FRILL OF IT

SONYA NIMRI

Photography by CARRIE GRIM * Illustrations by DANY PARAGOUTEVA

WATSON-GUPTILL PUBLICATIONS * NEW YORK

Senior Acquisitions Editor: **Julie Mazur**
Editor: **Cathy Hennessy**
Designer: **woolypear**
Production Manager: **Alyn Evans**

First published in 2007 by Watson-Guptill Publications, Nielsen Business Media, a division of The Nielsen Company
770 Broadway, New York, NY 10003
www.watsonguptill.com

Library of Congress Cataloging-in-Publication Data
Nimri, Sonya. Just for the frill of it : 25 flirty, fabulous styles to make with clothes you already own / by Sonya Nimri ;
photography by Carrie Grim ; illustrations by Dany Paragouteva.
p. cm.
Includes index.
ISBN-13: 978-0-8230-9997-9 (alk. paper)
ISBN-10: 0-8230-9997-0 (alk. paper)
1. Clothing and dress—Remaking. 2. Clothing and dress—Alteration. I. Title.
TT550.N56 2007
646.4'04—dc22 2007001285

Printed in Singapore

First printing, 2007

1 2 3 4 5 6 7 8 9 / 15 14 13 12 11 10 09 08 07

this book is dedicated to

MY DAD, who taught me to appreciate the overlooked, and

MY MOM, who taught me what to do with it.

contents

Introduction

No one needs this book. I'm sure you have clothes that are fine—they keep you warm when you're cold and cover up the necessary parts. But do you ever yearn for something more? Something that makes you stand out when you feel like a plain Jane, a little dose of personal style?

Do you own anything that no one else in the world has? (They say we all have a twin out there. Apparently people see mine all the time working out at my local gym—but I bet she doesn't have any of the clothes in this book!)

I have bigger ambitions than making a straight line when I sew; I want to make something that rocks. I want it to be unlike anything I've seen out there—a one-of-a-kind, original, Sonya-fied, inspired creation. A piece that comes forth from my brain, which is filled with the influences of street fashion, the runways of Paris, my travels around the world, my latest ideas and notions, and more. Mostly, I want to make something that is truly mine, something that I'm not seeing on the racks.

I remember when I was little, my friends and I would all get together and talk about the designs we were going to create when we grew up. I believe everyone has a designer inside of them. Each one of us has ideas about our personal style. We all know the shape of our favorite neckline, the skirt length that best suits our legs, the looks we like in magazines. Of course, that doesn't always translate into what we end up wearing, because it isn't always available. It's hard to find your style. But as far as creativity, and what we each want to look like, I am positive that you already know.

The process of making clothing is daunting, time-consuming, and scary. But the good news is that you don't need to start from scratch. Why spend time on shoulder seams, crotch construction, and other complicated details when there's a never-ending stockpile of clothes already in your closet, in thrift stores in your neighborhood, or hiding in your attic, just waiting for a pair of scissors to give them some style? This book shows you quick and easy ways to make something you may be a bit bored with into something you really love. Jump-start your style, and give these projects a whirl.

This book is designed to be a handbook of ideas, techniques, and inspiration. But don't stop here! Fashion is fun, and a great medium for self-expression. As you work through the projects, you may find that all sorts of other ideas start coming to you. Go with them! Don't let anything stop the creativity that starts flowing. So what if you cut too much material and ruin something? Just keep trying new things—it's all a learning process and you will know better for next time. Arm yourself with scissors, thread, and old clothes and go on an adventure you'll always remember.

note

Level of Difficulty

The 25 projects in this book each come complete with easy-to-follow step-by-steps that show how to use simple sewing, gluing, and embellishing to turn an old dud into a dream come true. The projects are rated by difficulty, so if you don't have a lot of time or are faced with a fashion emergency you'll be able to tell at a glance exactly which project will work for you. Look for the buttons at the top of the page to tell you the level of difficulty.

- **Easy as pie** (1 button)
- **Still mellow** (2 buttons)
- **A bit more intense** (3 buttons)
- **More of a commitment** (4 buttons)

GET INSPIRED!

Looking for fashion inspiration? Here are my favorite ways to get new design ideas:

1. **Go to stores you can't afford.**
   The reason some garments are more expensive than others is usually because it takes longer to make them or they are made with better-quality fabrics. I want the best of both worlds, so to avoid breaking the bank, I go to the stores I can't afford to check out the styles and cuts they offer, then I go to second-hand stores and pick up their finest quality garments, regardless of size or cut, and make them into my own tailored works of art. Sometimes I let the garment inspire me; other times, I have an idea in mind and look for a basic piece that fits the bill.

2. **Look to the haute couture collections.**
   Let geniuses of fashion, such as Vivien Westwood, John Galliano, and old-school designers such as Karl Lagerfeld, Christian Lacroix, and Valentino, show you the way. They all have very different styles, yet a consistent quality found only in haute couture. Their clothes are bold, bright, brazen, and always handmade.

3. **Take a museum day.**
   I love to go to museums and check out the paintings to see what people were wearing two hundred years ago. The color combinations, textures, styles—all are elements we have access to in our modern world, and yet I bet you no one else does that, except for Vivien and Karl, perhaps.

4. **Look around you.**
   Another great inspiration is street fashion. I always get ideas from what other mamas pull together. Go out to clubs and music festivals; even just walking down the street you'll see tons of interesting looks. There are so many girls out there with awesome style. Ladies, you just have to start checking each other out!

the Nitty-Gritty

What You Need to Get Started

There are a few essentials that you'll need for doing the projects in this book. They don't cost a fortune, and these basic tools will last you through many seasons of clothing transformations. A lot of this stuff you probably already have lying around the house or else can steal from your family's attic.

THE BASIC TOOLKIT

Scissors

There are a few types of scissors you'll need: first, a medium-sized (8- to 9-inch) pair to be used for fabric only. There is a trick to scissors that my dear mother taught me, which I am now going to pass on to you. When you buy fabric scissors, they need not be expensive. As a matter of fact, it doesn't really matter if you pay six bucks for them. (That's about how much mine were, and I've had them for ages.) The important thing is that they *must not be used on anything else besides fabric*. As soon as you cut a piece of paper, a plastic tag, a plastic six-pack holder, the scissors are finished and lose their sharpness. Save the seagulls with another pair of scissors, please.

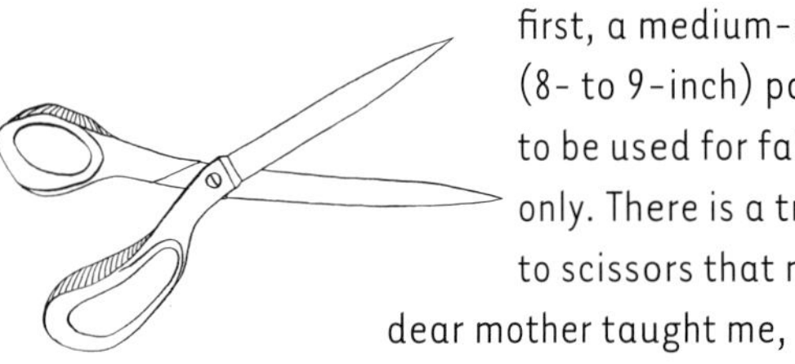

You'll also need a tiny pair of scissors (or embroidery scissors if you want to really go pro). A pair of nail scissors works fine, but my favorites are a pair shaped like a stork that I've seen in fabric stores everywhere. Little scissors are a must for cleaning up threads and raw edges, and evening out seams when your line is a bit crooked.

Finally, a pair of pinking shears. These aren't a necessity, but how cute is it when a raw edge is finished off with a zigzag instead of a straight line?

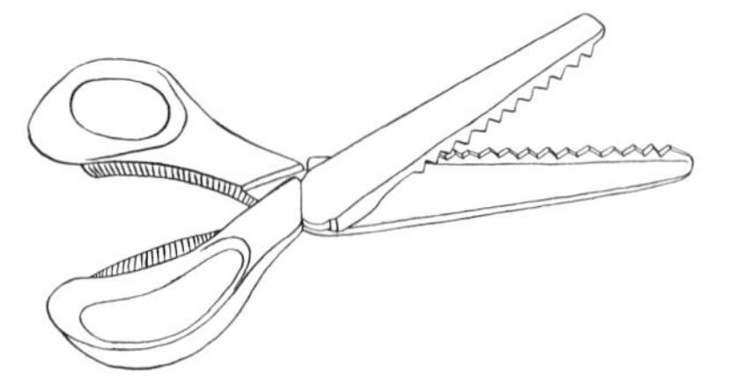

Thread

I recommend buying a basic starter set of thread—every local craft store carries them. The pack contains a variety of different colored threads on spools and bobbins. Believe it or not, thread actually rots. Thread is not the item to buy at a garage sale from Grandma Margie's Vintage Lot. Using old thread can single-handedly ruin a project, because the last thing you need is for your new hot pants to split up the crack after you down a chili cheese dog.

As for color, I recommend using thread as close as you can get to the color of the fabric on which you are sewing. For example, if you are sewing green ribbon onto a purple skirt, use green thread that is as close as possible to the shade of the ribbon. Also, when sewing on a machine, use thread from the same spool in the bobbin and the feeder. My late costume design teacher at UCLA, John Brandt, taught me this technique. He said that when thread comes from different sources, it has different tension properties that can mess up your machine's rhythm. I've never been a technically savvy girl, but this makes a certain amount of sense to me. He also used to throw bent needles on the floor in disgust and climb out of bathroom windows with James Dean, but that is another story . . .

When in a pinch, if you have, say, only black and white thread and are sewing a yellow skirt, use the closest color—in this case, white. I went through a stage where I was deliberately trying to make the thread color contrasting, and I can tell you, it never really worked. It just looked sort of amateurish. Of course, sometimes I can't be bothered to change the bobbin from my last project, and it doesn't match, but well, c'est la vie!

Needles

I like to keep a range of different sized needles around. I like the long, thin ones for tacking and sewing long running stitches, and the short ones for sewing on buttons. You can buy a pack with different sized needles at the craft store for a couple of bucks and they last a long time unless they break, which rarely happens.

Straight Pins

Sometimes I'm lazy about pinning my work together before I sew it down. I must admit, it is a problem, because I'm usually trying to save time and what I end up doing is sewing crooked lines, tearing the seam out, and redoing it anyway, which takes even more time. So . . . pin, pin, pin your work down before sewing it! My mom goes so far as to tack it in place, which is a really loose hand-sew, to make sure it works before the final stitch. I find this approach a bit too much—pinning doesn't take nearly as long, and is a must.

Pins that get trampled by the machine and bent out of shape must be thrown out immediately. They twist your work around and can ruin a perfectly good pinning job by offsetting the line. Stick the ends of the pins in bubble gum before throwing them in the trash to keep them from poking out and piercing the garbageman's delicate arms.

Pincushion

A pincushion is a necessity. As you are sewing your piece, you will be removing the pins and will need something to stick them into. Don't ever let them fall on the floor. There is nothing more painful than running for the phone and stepping on a pin that is sticking straight up! It's happened to me a few times, and believe me, your foot will throb for days. So stick your pins into something—anything, really. Sometimes I can't find my cushion and use rolls of duct tape, the drapes, stuffed animals, junk mail, or plastic bottles—they all work just as well.

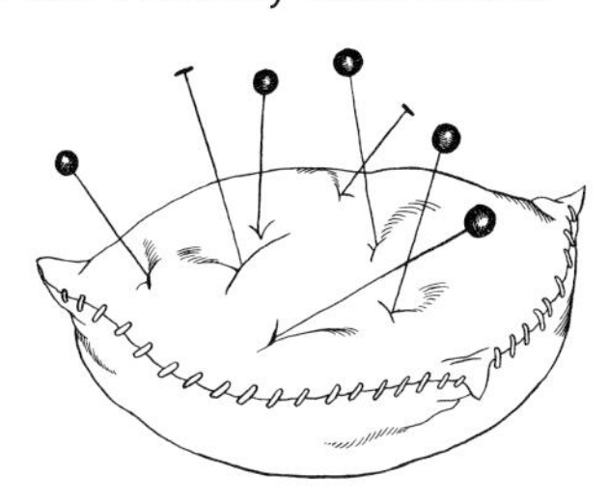

Seamstress Tape

Seamstress tape is essential for making sure your measurements are even. Believe it or not, even lines are the key to a professional-looking piece.

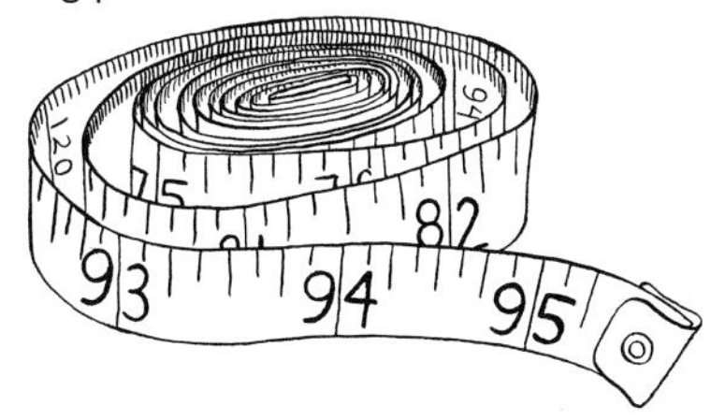

Fabric Pencil

A fabric pencil (also known as tailor's chalk) is great for marking up where you want to cut your garment. The nice thing about it is that the marks come out in the wash, so you don't have to worry about making mistakes.

Seam Ripper

For me, much of garment construction is actually taking apart a piece that I find restricting—meaning I like to tear out seams. Somehow you can drastically change a garment simply by ripping open a seam and then resewing it slightly differently. Seam rippers also come in handy when I make a mistake and must rip out a seam I just made (which never happens, wink wink). I use this tool almost as often as I use my needle and thread, and consider it one of my top five must-haves.

Iron and Ironing board

When redoing existing pieces, you'll sometimes find creases that have been in the fabric for generations. It would be great if we could just snap our fingers and say, "Pleats be gone!" but it's not quite that easy. Sometimes it takes a spritz of water and a lot of ironing.

If you don't have an ironing board, a towel works in a pinch. But I prefer the little boards that expand on a table. I don't have a full, freestanding model because it would never fit in my tiny apartment, but the tabletop model is adequate for our needs.

Fray Check

Many designers these days,from Karl L. to Johnny G., leave raw edges. I don't know if they let their pants whittle away into knickers, but I like to seal edges from fraying further with Fray Check™. All you have to do to seal a raw edge is dab this alcohol-smelling solution on a frayed edge and let it dry. A few minutes later, the edge is stiff as a board and won't fray your seam away. It changes the look of the fibers a bit and turns them a bit prickly looking, but it saves hours of sewing and keeps the intended seam of your piece intact. Fray Check™ is machine-washable and dry-cleanable but is not intended for pieces that will be thrown into the washing machine every week. I use it mostly on shoe clips, purses, hair accessories, belts, ribbon, lace, and detachable collars.

GARMENTS THAT ARE GAME

May I start off by saying, please, *don't* start from scratch with your sewing projects. Making your clothes from scratch is so passé. It died with eight-tracks and stirrup pants, hopefully never to return. Why waste your time when there is so much mass-produced raw material out there, waiting to be transformed into magical, personality-filled garments that only you possess? Before I got hip to the scissors methodology, I was an okay seamstress, but I can't tell you how many times I thought, "There must be an easier way." It was super-frustrating, and the pieces never turned out the way I'd imagined (of course, it could also mean that I'm impatient and stink at sewing). Plus, there are so many things I would rather be doing—dancing, seeing my favorite band, riding my bike on the beach, eating prosciutto and melon in Venice, and then getting a quadruple scoop of gelato . . .

Garments come in a variety of weights and textures, and different pieces are good for different projects. After you experiment a bit, you'll see what I'm talking about. Most of the projects in this book are made from very common shapes and varieties of sweaters, tank tops, T-shirts, scarves, and skirts.

An amazing fact about most machine-knit clothes is that they don't unravel like a ball of yarn. Cut off the bottom of a sleeve and try pulling on a random thread, and you will notice that it just doesn't unravel. This weird fact means that you can cut up any machine-knit piece and it won't fall apart—making them perfect victims for reconstruction.

This book focuses on knits made of cotton, cashmere, wool, and silk. Synthetics like acrylic, rayon, and spandex work just as well, but I tend to prefer natural fibers; I find that they breathe better and look très chic. But that's only my opinion—basically, anything machine-knit is fair game.

Here is a list of basic clothing items to start collecting:

Tank Tops

A cotton tank top is the perfect candidate for a makeover. I've included three simple and dramatic ways to transform these boring basics into something a bit more rock-and-roll: Laced with Charm, the Naughty See's Candy Lady, and Buttoned Up.

Tank tops come both ribbed and nonribbed. I prefer ribbed numbers because the ribbing lets me count spaces when weaving ribbon through the tank top at the collar or on the sides. Of course, a ruler does the same thing—I just like things as easy as possible, and anyone who knows me knows that I am bad with numbers.

Jersey-Knit Shirts

These are the shirts you wish you didn't have to own. They're the kind of tight and very boring work shirts that you wear with slacks for a job interview. When you've gotten the job and decide it's time to kick back and party, tear this shirt into a low-cut flirtatious number for late-night seduction. In this book, projects like the Fräulein Über-Vamp and Lacy/DC tops show how different your final creations can look.

Sweaters

Sweaters are prime candidates for tearing apart because sometimes it's just way too hot in there! Especially with cowl-neck, turtleneck, or V-neck sweaters, I often find I get so hot that I just want to rip them off.

I know I can't be the only one who feels this way, although I do live in California. Sweaters are perfect for cutting up anyhow, because their weighty material helps them keep their shape.

Scarves

Scarves are available in thrift stores everywhere, as well as your mom's and grandma's closets. I bought all the scarves in this book for a dollar each at the Rose Bowl Flea Market, a gigantic outdoor market at a football stadium in Pasadena. The scarves for Swing Around the Posy, Le St. Tropez, and Copacabana, plus the trim on the Tango Top, were all Rose Bowl scores. I usually prefer light silk scarves of Indian origin for trim (Tango Top), but for the St. Tropez and Copacabana projects, I chose design and thickness over softness of thread, and went with 1960s–1970s polyester scarves. They are durable enough for a night of dancing, keep their shape a bit better, and are easy to hand-wash.

Old Purses

These are not, technically, clothing, but purses are great for redo projects, especially when they are stained or torn in a conspicuous spot. A friend of mine gave me a satin purse that had a coffee stain running down it—I glued feathers to it and voilà, I had created Opposite Feathers, shown on page 94 to inspire you.

THE SKINNY ON SWEATER WEIGHTS

Knits generally come in a variety of weights. Three common ones you will find referred to in this book are *fingering, sport weight,* and *worsted weight*. This won't be on the label, but you can eyeball your finds for an estimate. Here's a little primer on each.

Fingering Weight

This is the very thin-weight sweater that you see those high-society ladies wearing over their shoulders with big pearl necklaces and button-down collared shirts (think Babs Bush). I love finding these pieces at the Salvation Army; they usually have a Worcestershire sauce stain on them, or a few moth holes (which is why no one else has scooped them up). These small flaws can be easily fixed with a lace or velveteen patch and sometimes the stain or the hole is below the line where the new hem will be, so it will end up getting cut out anyway. The fingering-weight projects in this book are the Frilled and Fabulous shrug and Frilled and Fabulous Pooch jacket.

Sport Weight

Sport-weight sweaters are the kind that city girls wear in the spring when it starts to get warm, but not quite warm enough for a sundress. Examples in this book are the Tango Top and the Granny Bolero. The Tango Top was made from a wool Benetton V-neck that I picked up in Europe and never wore because it was so hot, a bit too small, and tight at the neck. The Granny Bolero was made from a cotton granny cardigan I picked up at a thrift store.

Worsted Weight

This is the standard American winter sweater weight—twice the thickness of sport weight—and the most common weight you will find. This book's worsted-weight projects include Highland Lass and Let's Get Physical, both made from sweaters I wore for a couple of seasons before growing bored with their shapes. It happens—what can I say?

WHERE TO FIND CLOTHES TO MAKE OVER

Your Own Closet

Look for clothes you are planning to get rid of anyway or never wear. It's like shopping for free.

Your Best Friend's Closet

Hunt for clothes you haven't seen her wear in ages and see if she'll turn them over to you.

Goodwill, the Salvation Army, Garage Sales, Swap Meets

These can be great resources, whether you have a specific project in mind or are just looking for a sweater to jump up and tell you it wants to be yours. Of course, always sniff it first.

THE ICING ON THE CAKE

Your makeover project is a lot like a cake. The better stocked your cupboard is, the easier it is to arrive at a fantastic end result without leaving the house. I am a big proponent of collecting a stash of supplies for your great works of art—the good thing about starting a collection is that many times it doesn't cost a thing. A bit of lace from a ripped nightgown, ribbons from birthday or Christmas presents, old costume jewelry—and suddenly you have the makings of a great collection. Here are some things to keep an eye out for:

Junk Jewelry

About six months ago, I inherited a pile of really hideous junk jewelry from my boyfriend's stepdad's mother. My friends and I were doubled over in laughter as we pawed through it, splitting the spoils and wondering what we were going to do with it all. Believe it or not, I've used so much of it in this book! Who knew? One terrible clunky rope necklace was stitched to a classic black dress to create Mademoiselle Coco (page 88). Another necklace I took apart to bead onto the handle of Opposite Feathers (page 94). An accordion slinky '80s deal was used for the collar of the Copacabana (page 114), and the funniest one of all, a chain-link choker she must have innocently worn with a sweater set, became the dog collar in Frilled and Fabulous Pooch (page 46).

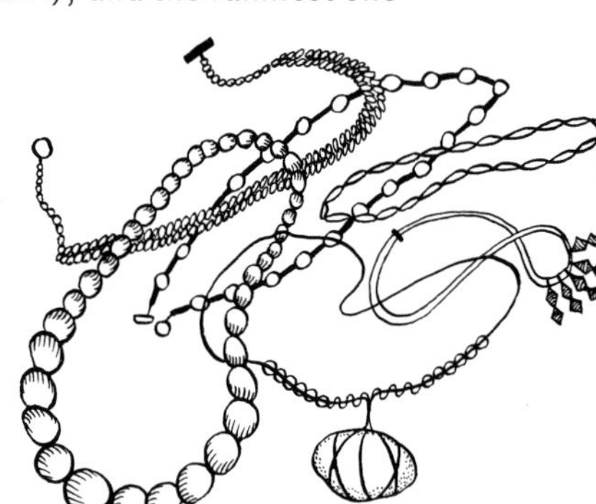

Buttons, Ribbons, Feathers, and Lace
I'm lucky to live in Los Angeles, which has a lively, well-stocked garment district where costume designers can pick up supplies for everything from alien costumes to Vegas showgirl numbers and period pieces. I tried to limit myself to supplies that would be available everywhere, although if you live in a remote area, it's all available online (see pages 127 for a list of websites and other resources).

Lace trim is easy to find at fabric stores in the bridal section; you can also buy lace fabric by the yard and convert it into trim by cutting it to the width you need. Feather trim attached to ribbon is available by the yard at some craft stores and on the Internet. Feather boas can be made into trim by folding a 1-inch-wide ribbon lengthwise over the boa's string binding and hot-gluing it together.

I also paw through thrift store jackets, shirts, and accessories for buckles, buttons, bits of lace, and ribbon that can be removed and converted into great accents. The variety of ribbon seems ever expanding at craft stores these days—I think it has something to do with the scrapbooking craze—and is great for clothing renegades everywhere.

Grommets
Available at the hardware store, these round metal rings are the final touch on the Let's Get Physical sweater's collar (page 38). Attaching grommets requires a hammer and a steady hand, but they add a professional look to clothing. I recommend practicing on spare fabric first because if you mess one up, there is nothing to do but cut your mistake off or put in a bigger grommet.

Fabric Samples
The Shabby Chic Belt makes use of three vintage (meaning from my parents' attic) upholstery fabric samples that came from some reupholstering shop in the 1970s. Fabric samples can come in very handy—they're available at fabric stores, or ask a reupholstering shop if they have spare scraps they can donate for a very chic cause.

Basic techniques

Sewing is not as scary as it looks. If it were, there wouldn't be kits in every hotel room in the world for the average guest to use if his/her button falls off or pants rip in the crotch. Sewing is as easy as pulling a needle back and forth through a piece of fabric in a repetitive, even motion. It can even be very relaxing at times. Here are the techniques used in this book to get you started.

SEWING BY HAND

If you've never used a sewing machine before, or just don't have one, hand-sewing is a good way to dip your toes into the sewing pool. Hand-sewing gives you more control over what you're doing. Some things can only be sewn on by hand, like buttons, hooks and eyes, and snaps. Other things, like appliqués (where you sew a bit of lace or fabric on top of another), look better when sewn on by hand, unless you're really good on the sewing machine. Hand-sewing is also the best way to make a hem if you want a seamless look, with no threads showing.

Anything done on a sewing machine can also be sewn by hand—it's just slower. For projects with delicate bits of lace, like Laced with Charm, Naughty See's Candy Lady, Mademoiselle Coco, and Ruffled Around the Edges, it is much easier to sew by hand than to use a machine because that way, you have more control over the needle.

HAND-SEWING 101

Threading a Needle

No idea how to start? The first step to any hand-sewing is to get your thread on the needle.

1. Take a piece of thread, about 2 feet long, and a needle.

2. Moisten one end of the thread and roll it between your fingertips to create a point.

3. Poke the pointed end through the eye of the needle.

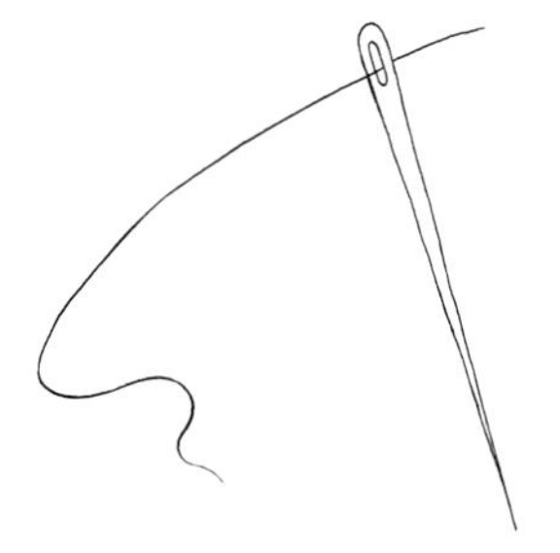

4. Pull so that the thread is doubled and even in length. Make a knot at the end.

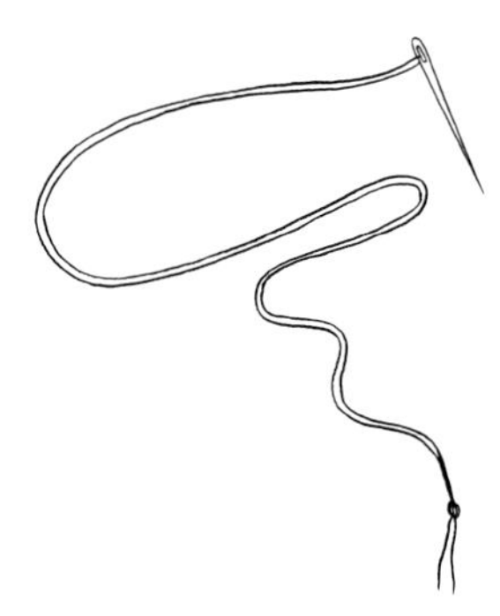

Running Stitch

This stitch does not stretch out, which makes it good for keeping pieces of ribbon and lace right where you want them. It's the hand version of the straight stitch on a machine.

1. Poke your needle through the fabric from back to front, so the knot and tail are hidden on the underside.

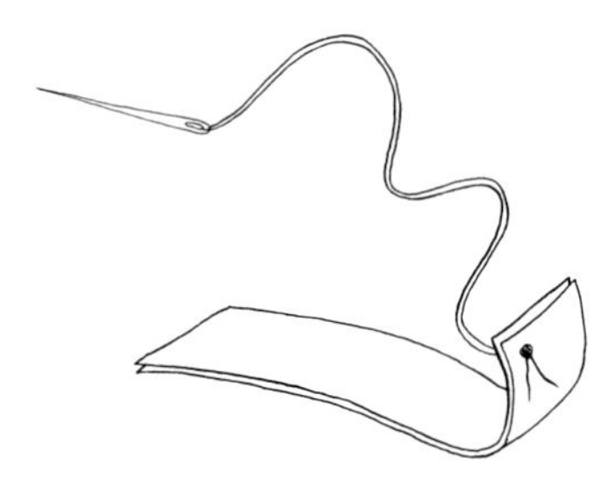

2. Moving in a straight line, poke your needle back through to the underside about 1/8 inch away from where it came out in step 1.

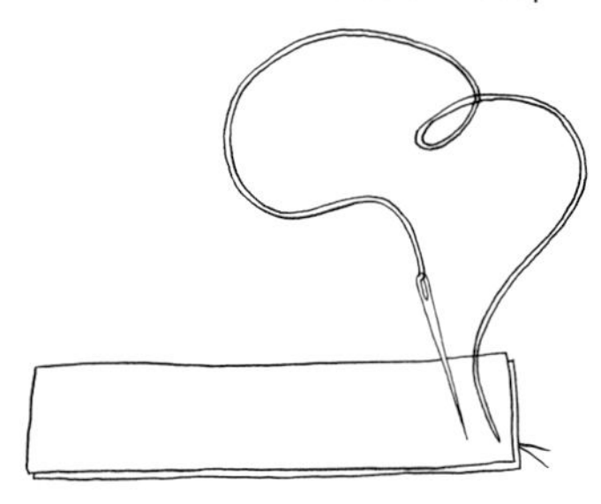

3. Repeat steps 1–2, moving in as straight a line as possible and keeping your stitches spaced about 1/8 inch apart.

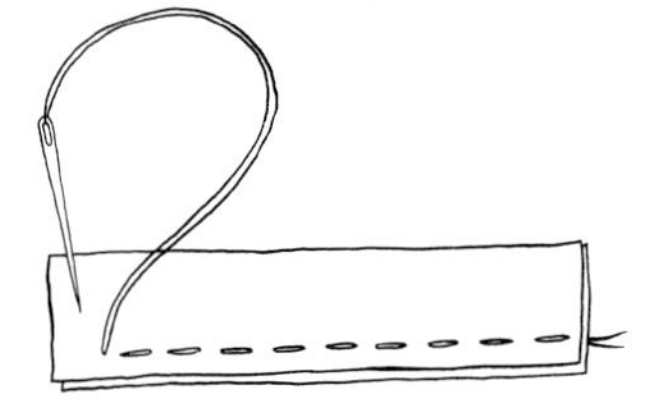

4. When you're finished, tie off as for the whipstitch.

Basting Stitch

This is just a looser version of the running stitch. Space the stitches every ¼ inch (instead of every ⅛ inch), and keep it all very loose so the fabric can be pulled on the thread and gathered into a ruffle.

Whipstitch

This is the stitch I use most when hand-sewing because it allows fabric to stretch and to move with you.

1. Fold over your hem or roll the edge so that the raw edge is tucked in.

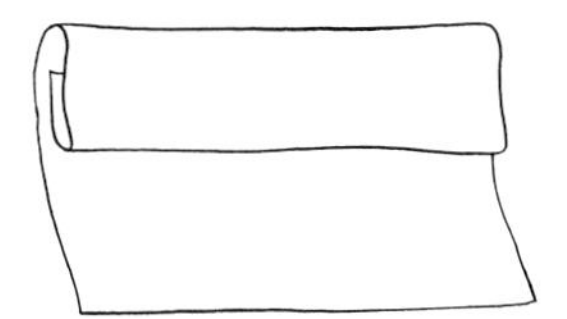

2. Find an inconspicuous place to start, where the knot will be tucked into the seam and hidden from view.

3. Poke your needle through and pull it through all desired layers without penetrating the outside layers of the garment. Pull taut but do not pull too tightly or the thread will break when the seam is stretched.

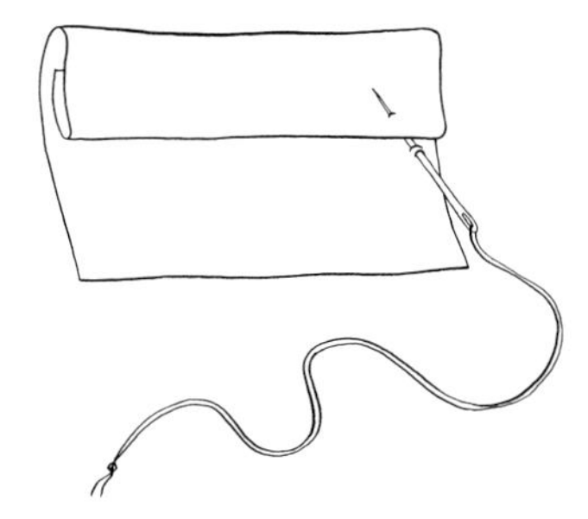

4. Move about ⅛ inch from your first stitch and repeat step 3, running the needle in the same direction.

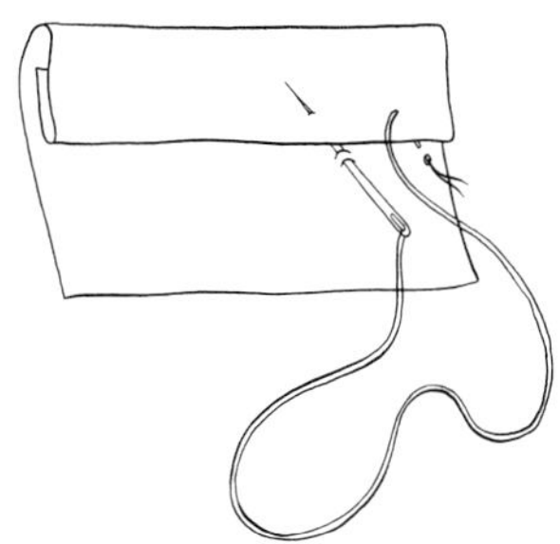

5. Keep making stitches until you either finish or run out of thread. If you have finished stitching, skip to step 6. If you run out of thread before the hem is finished, thread the needle again and keep going.

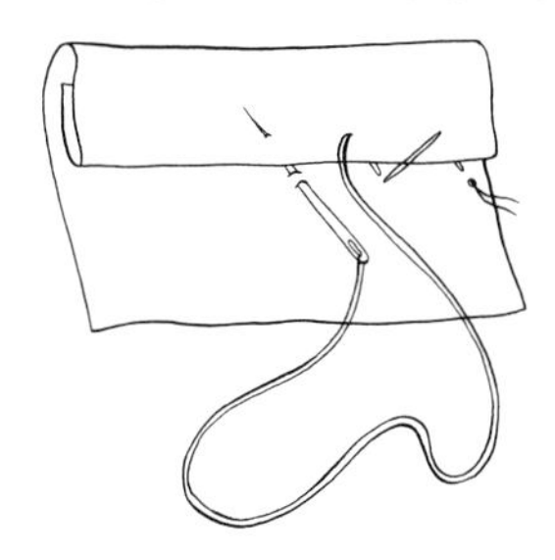

6. To finish, pull your needle and thread a few times through the last stitch to reinforce it. Cut the thread, leaving a 3- or 4-inch tail. Tie the two tail pieces together a couple times to secure, then trim off the extra thread.

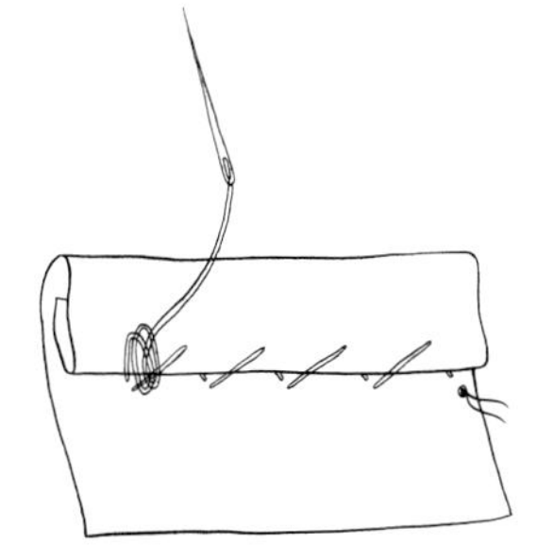

Zigzag Stitch

This is the stitch I use most on the machine when finishing edges; it can also be achieved by hand.

1. Starting at the underside of the fabric, poke the needle through to the front.
2. Moving in a diagonal line, poke the needle back down about $^1/_8$ inch away from the first hole. You are creating a slanted stitch.

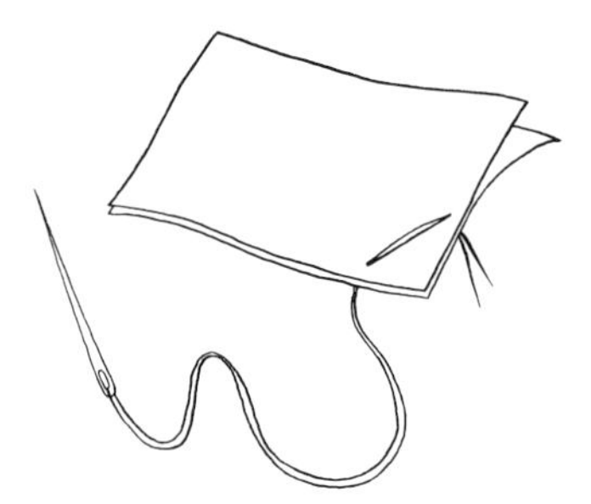

3. Poke the needle back up right next to the first down stitch.

4. Poke the needle back down, at an angle diagonal to where it came up, in order to have two stitches that look like a V.

5. Repeat steps 1–4 until the end of your line.

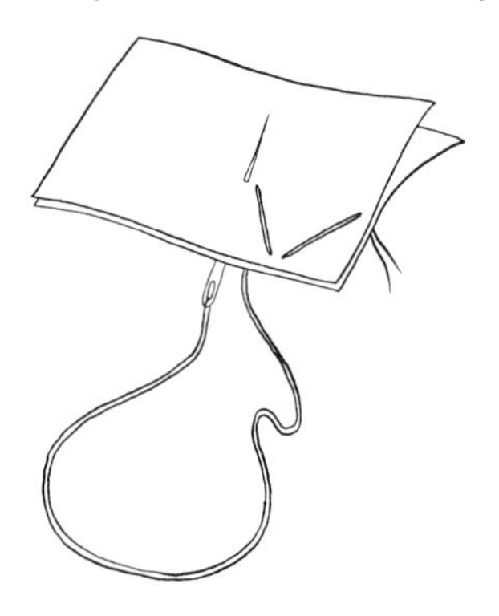

MACHINE SEWING

Machine sewing is the fastest and easiest way to finish hems and attach two pieces of fabric together. If you've never sewn before, practice at least a dozen or so lines of different stitches on a scrap piece of fabric before attempting your masterpiece—sometimes a stitch can go wild and take forever to rip out and redo. Read the instruction manual carefully and figure out how to thread your machine. Threading your machine is key, so practice about eight times until you get the hang of it. A badly threaded machine will make a bad stitch that will definitely have to be torn out.

Go slow when you sew. It's not a race to the finish. It's more important that it be well done and not a sloppy mess. Your work is a reflection of you, so you want it to be top-notch!

Zigzag Stitch

The zigzag stitch enables fabric to move freely and to expand and contract. It's great for any seam you want to stretch with you as you move, which includes most of the seams in this book. One thing to figure out is how big you want to make the stitch. The range on the sewing machine is from 0 to 6: the bigger the number, the bigger and looser the stitch. The thickness of what you are sewing should usually determine the size of your stitch. Thicker fabrics need a bigger stitch or they will pucker and look strange, while thinner fabrics work best with a smaller zigzag.

Straight Stitch

The straight stitch is great for sewing something you don't want to expand or stretch out, like a collar or a decorative ribbon. Another advantage of the straight stitch is that it does not obscure the design on the ribbon (as a zigzag stitch would), so your focus stays on the ribbon and not on the stitch. The tension (a setting on your sewing machine) is something you will have to experiment with here, because depending on your ribbon and sweater chemistry, the stitch will differ.

ADDING NEW FABRIC TO EXISTING PIECES

When you add new fabric to an existing garment there are three different ways of sewing the seams together: face-to-face, old overlapping new, or new overlapping old.

Face-to-Face

This is the most common way. The two fabrics are laid on top of each other like an inside-out sandwich, with the reverse sides facing out and the "right" sides facing each other on the inside. The seam is sewn and then the sandwich is turned right-side out, thus hiding the seam.

Old Overlapping New

Another technique is to overlap the "old" fabric over the new and sew the seam on the outside. This gives your piece a rougher, deliberately raw look. I used this technique in the Granny Bolero to counter the original sweater's innately conservative look.

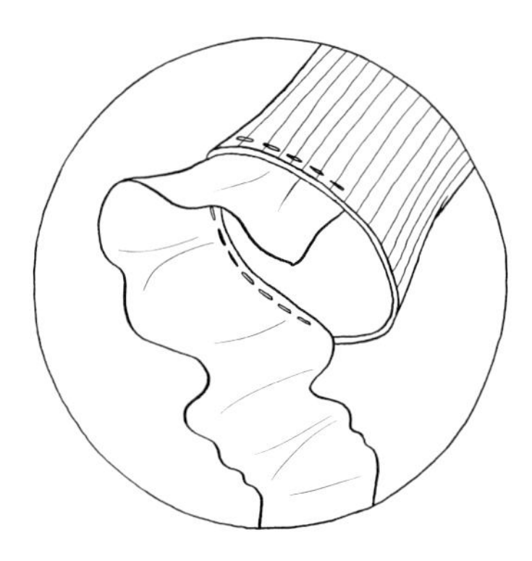

New Overlapping Old

This technique highlights the new fabric the most because none of it is hidden. It creates a heavier, more substantial-looking hem and is ideal for maximum frill, as in the Frilled and Fabulous Pooch.

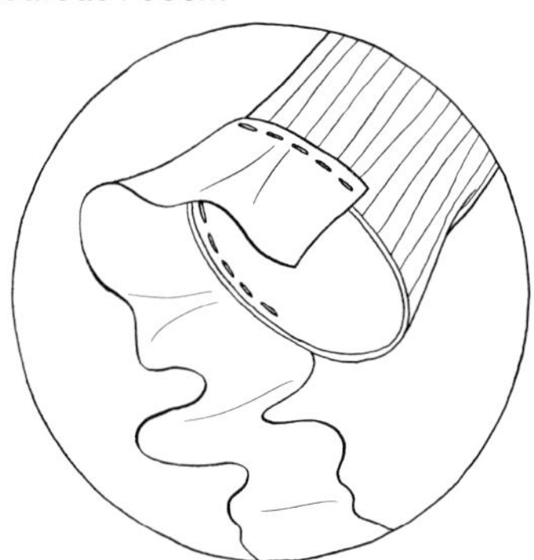

TIP

Seam Allowance

When creating a seam, there is always the question of how much fabric to leave on the inside of the stitch, also called the seam allowance. *I like to leave between 1/4 inch and 1/2 inch.*

NONSEWING ALTERNATIVES

For those of you who are really averse to sewing, a variety of products on the market provide temporary or permanent ways to attach fabric without sewing. These products can work well for adhering embellishments to clothing, but I would not recommend them for structural changes to a garment, such as adding part of a sleeve or adding a ruffle to the bottom of a hem.

Fabric Glue

Several different types of fabric glue are on the market. Glues for attaching rhinestones, sequins, glitter, and gems to fabric are made in both washable (permanent) and nonwashable formulas. Some fabric glues form a permanent bond between two layers of fabric—a sort of liquid fusible web that can be used in no-sew projects. There is also specialized "stretchable" fabric glue for adding ornamentation to stretchable fabrics.

Bonding Fabric or Fusible Web

Another type of fabric adhesive is iron-on bonding fabric, sometimes called "fusible web." This layer of adhesive material is placed between two layers of "regular" fabric to fuse them together permanently. It comes in tape and sheets, with or without backing paper. Some fusible webbing has pressure-sensitive adhesive on both sides to hold items temporarily in place before they are ironed to fuse them together.

Fusible web in tape form can be used for hemming. Tape widths range from 1/4 inch to 1 1/4 inches. To hem with fusible web, place it between the hem allowance and the garment or other item, setting it down a bit from the edge of the hem allowance. Pin it and then iron according to directions. For heavy material, a wider strip (up to the depth of the hem allowance) is used to give the hem more strength.

Fusible Interfacing

Fusible interfacing includes fabric adhesive already bonded to a material. Both regular and sculpting-woven interfacing are available in fusible versions, along with nonwoven styles. Fusible interfacing can be used for garments, window shade backing, handbags, and other projects. It also comes in a variety of materials, including tricot, 100% polyester, and various polyester/nylon blends, as well as in specialized forms for different fabric weights.

Snaps

Snaps are another way to avoid or at least limit sewing. Depending on the type, they can be applied with a hammer or sewn on, and are sold in strips on a ribbon or individually. You can apply one side of the snaps on a strip to the bottom of a garment on which you want to attach something, and then apply the other side of the snap row to the material you want to attach. This makes the parts detachable in case you decide to change them. For example, you may want to have several types of trim for a sweater.

OTHER TECHNIQUES THAT ROCK

Weaving Ribbon

Weaving ribbon through fabric is a quick way to create a really cute effect in literally minutes. If you're weaving in and out of a sweater (see Highland Lass), you can simply attach your ribbon to a safety pin and use that to weave the ribbon through. For more tightly woven knits, such as a ribbed tank top (see Laced with Charm), the key is to use an upholstery needle so you won't break threads as you weave the ribbon through. Just make sure your needle has an eye that's large enough to fit your ribbon.

For a sweater, secure the ends by tying the ribbon with a knot to the knitting. If you're working with a tighter weave, either tie the ribbon to itself in a bow, or tie the ribbon to itself and then make a knot.

Ruffling Fabric

Creating a ruffled edge is easy—it's done by slightly pleating or bunching one piece of fabric while sewing it to another.

Make sure you have extra material for the ruffled edging. If you want a really thick, wavy ruffle, you'll need a piece of fabric that's at least double the length of the edge you are sewing it to. For a smaller ruffle, you'll need a piece one and a half times the length of the edge. Before you start, always measure out the amount of fabric you have to work with to be sure it's enough. Sometimes I cut the fabric lengthwise to create double the ruffling material.

To create the ruffle, pin your fabric along the edge, bunching it as you go. The bigger and closer together you make the bunches, the fuller and wavier the ruffle. For a fuller ruffle, I usually bunch it every $1/4$ inch or so, overlapping the fabric a great deal for each bunch; for a smaller ruffle, I make a little bunch every inch or so.

It's a good idea to pin the ruffle in place first, to make sure it stays consistently wavy along the whole edge. Sometimes if I don't do this, I end up ruffling too much at the beginning and then running out of fabric at the other side.

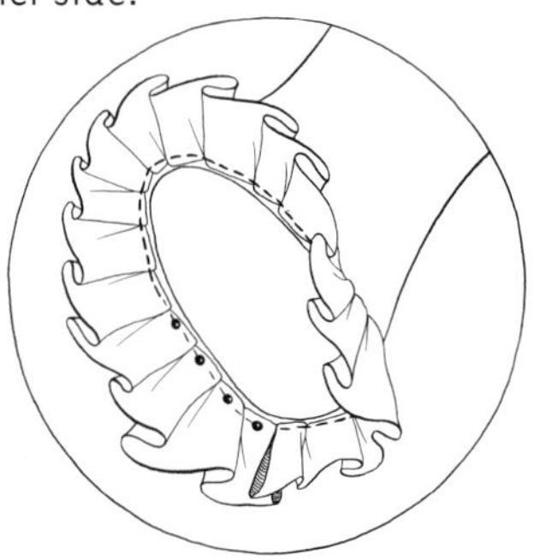

Another way to create a ruffle is to sew a loose basting stitch (see page 27) along the edge of the fabric to be ruffled, and then pull the fabric so it gathers along the thread. Adjust the fabric along the thread so that it is evenly gathered, then knot the thread at the end of the line. Place the ruffle where you intend to sew it down, then pin it in place to ensure that it does not shift around.

WHERE TO RUSTLE UP RUFFLES

Sometimes I use scarves to create ruffled edges, as in the Tango Top and Swing Around the Posy. Other times I want the ruffle to have a raw edge, so I use ripped strips of fabric. To rip fabric correctly, make a snip into the edge where you want to rip, aligning your snip with the "grain" of the fabric (the way the threads are running). Then rip the fabric down from your snip. This is what the salesperson does at the fabric store when you buy fabric with a straight weave. Don't do this with anything delicate, like lace or mesh, because it won't tear in a straight line and must be cut with scissors.

Using Fray Check

When using ripped strips of fabric, it is necessary to apply Fray Check to the edges so they don't continue to fray and shed threads all over the place. I used Fray Check in Fräulein Über-Vamp and General Plaid Regalia. See page 18 for more on Fray Check.™

note

A Word About Gluing

Hot-gluing (or any kind of gluing) is never a substitute for sewing on garments, because it is not washable, and your creations will fall apart with all the movement a young lady must make to get through the day. I cringe at the thought of my lace appliqué falling off my body as I walk through the farmer's market on Saturday morning. Hot gluing is, however, a great technique for accessories, like the Opposite Feathers, Queen Victoria's Tea Party Toes, General Plaid Regalia, and the Pansies Purse.

Dyeing

Dyeing clothes is a good way to transform something that is great in all aspects besides color, to something that is just all-around great. It's super-easy, too, and there is no lack of color choices or levels of difficulty. For quick dyeing tips and tons of information on the subject, go to www.ritdye.com.

CARING FOR YOUR NEW THREADS

Embellished clothes tend to be a little more delicate than they were before, because they are now combinations of different elements—jewelry, feathers, ribbons, silk scarves, and neckties. To prevent colors from bleeding, the safest way to go is to have your new garment dry-cleaned. Daddy's Girl, Mademoiselle Coco, and Frilled and Fabulous are three pieces that absolutely must be dry-cleaned—chains will rust if thrown in the wash, silk will do all sorts of funky things, and bright trims run the risk of tainting lighter clothing.

If you want to take a chance with the other garments—and I say that only because there is always a risk of colors bleeding—you should try hand-washing them. I hand-wash all my sweaters and never have a problem with them coming apart or color bleeding. Anything involving a scarf can also be hand-washed, although if it's silk, the washing might soften up the fibers and give it a peach-fuzz look. Dry cleaning will keep fabrics intact.

All the accessories in this book can be hand-washed if they get stained; the Duct-taped and Dangerous purse can just be hosed down.

ready

set

FRILL!

sweaters

Let's Get Physical

This was one of those sweaters that made me so hot I just had to cut it up. I remember wearing it out and sweating in it in zero-degree weather. It is one of those thermal knit numbers from Ireland that was designed for an Arctic expedition. Well, I was about to give it to the less fortunate when I looked at it, thought about how I loved the vibrant kelly green color, and grabbed my scissors. Too cute to donate, too warm to wear . . . the rest is history.

WHAT YOU'LL NEED

- **Sport-weight pullover sweater in wool or a synthetic fiber**
- **Scissors**
- **Tiny nail scissors or embroidery scissors**
- **2 grommets and grommet setting tool (often sold with the grommets)**
- **Hammer**
- **Needle and thread**
- **Fabric pencil**
- **Sewing machine (optional)**

DIRECTIONS

1. Put the sweater on and mark where you want the bottom of the bolero to fall. Do the same for the sleeves. Take the sweater off. Using your marks as guides, cut straight across the bottom. Cut the sleeves on a diagonal.

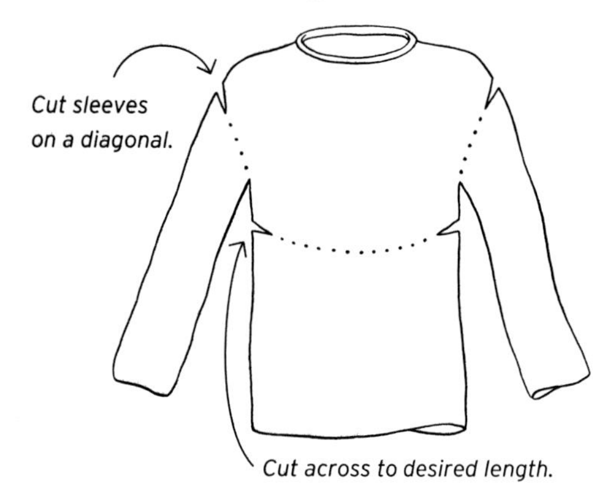

2. Cut down the center of the *front only*, creating a cardigan.

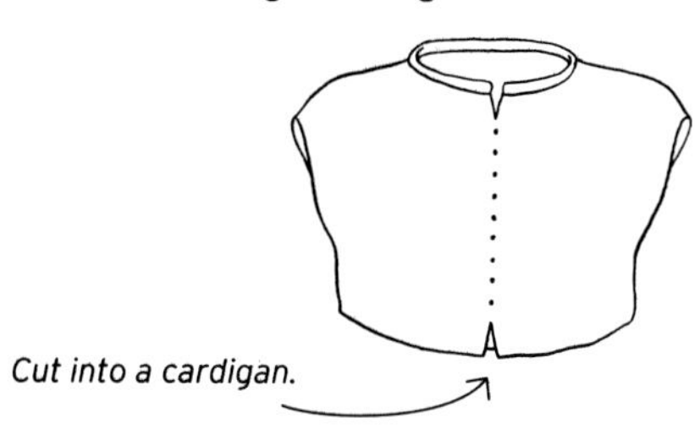

3. Starting an inch down from the collar, make a 1-inch horizontal cut, then swoop in and down with the scissors to create a bolero shape, ending at the seam.

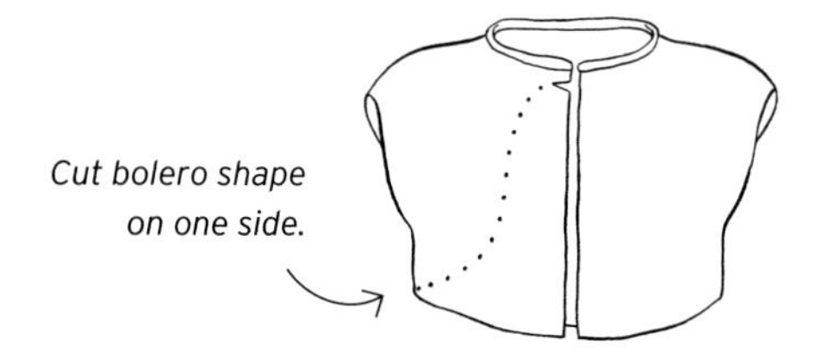

4. Take the cutout and lay it across the other side of the sweater, using it as a stencil to cut the same shape on that side.

5. Use your tiny scissors to make a small hole in one side of the front collar flap. Put the grommet through the hole and set it with a hammer (follow the directions on the package). Repeat on the opposite collar flap at exactly the same place.

6. Hem the armholes using a zigzag stitch, stretching each armhole as you go.

7. Hem the raw sweater edge, starting at the collar and using a zigzag stitch.

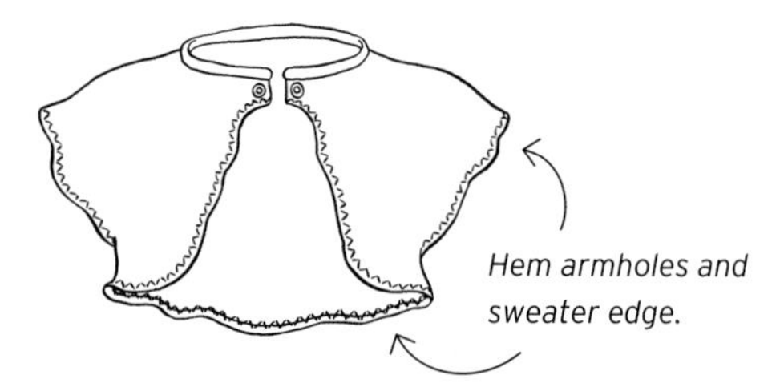

TOP 10 THINGS TO DO WHILE WEARING

Let's Get Physical

1. Join a gym.
2. Roller skate!
3. Make your best friend a headband and matching wrist bands from the scraps of this project.
4. Watch *Xanadu* with Olivia Newton-John.
5. Learn a recipe for oatbran muffins.
6. Fake a leg cramp so a cute boy will help you massage it out.
7. Throw out your rowing machine and buy a yoga mat.
8. Call your mom and tell her you think she is in great shape for her age. Ask for her fitness secrets.
9. Walk instead of driving somewhere.
10. Wash your car.

Variation

The shape of this sweater is completely up to you. It doesn't need to be a bolero—it can be a blunt, square shape; a scalloped shape; or you can leave it longer. The beauty of using scissors is that you can get creative and make the shape your own.

Frilled and Fabulous

WHAT YOU'LL NEED

- **Long-sleeved, fingering-weight stretchy sweater in wool or cashmere. (A cotton or synthetic sweater won't work because the fibers do not stretch enough.)**
- **2 yards of lace for trim, 3 inches wide**
- **2 yards of decorative embroidered ribbon, ½ inch wide**
- **Straight pins**
- **Scissors**
- **Needle and thread and/or sewing machine**

When I was a little girl, I always loved old ladies in cashmere sweater sets. My dad used to drive a group of such ladies to church every Sunday, and I remember sitting on their laps, afraid to put all my weight down for fear of hurting their meatless thighs with my bony bum. I remember their perfumes as well: Youth Dew *(the irony),* *Yves Saint Laurent's* Opium, *and Jean Patou's* Joy. *This is a great project for reviving a sweater that, once upon a time, was worn by a genteel belle to church on Sundays.*

DIRECTIONS

1. Cut the sweater in a bolero shape, as shown. It's easiest to start by cutting off the collar, about ¼ inch below the neckline. Then cut around the neckline and curve down toward the back. Cropping the bottom right at the elbow mark is a good place for the hem.

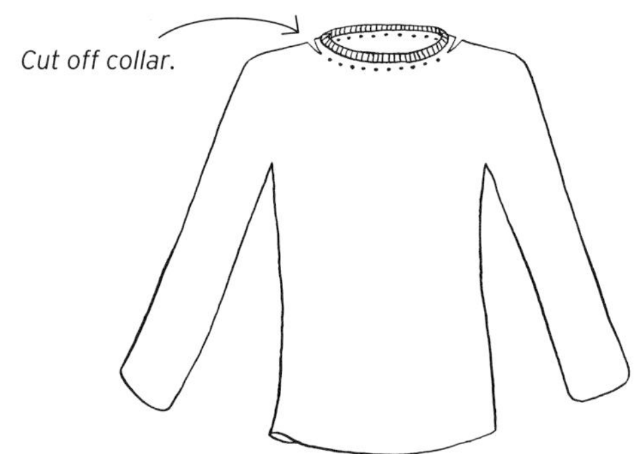

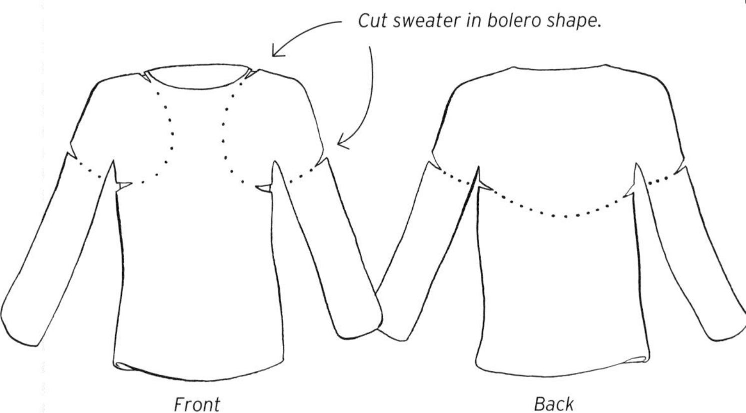

2. Stretch out the armholes as far as they will go.

3. Hand-finish the sleeve bottoms by turning the raw edge under twice, then hem with a whipstitch.

4. Pin lace trim all around the raw edge on the inside, bunching it every ¼ inch to create a ruffle. Try not to stretch out the collar. Machine or hand-sew down lace and remove pins.

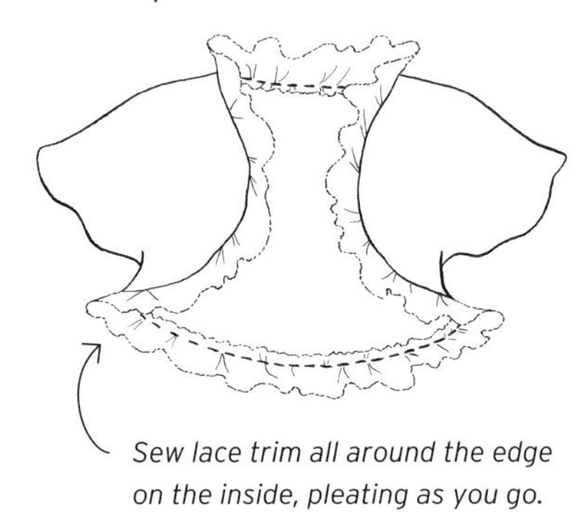

5. Sew ribbon all along the sweater edge on the outside, by hand or machine.

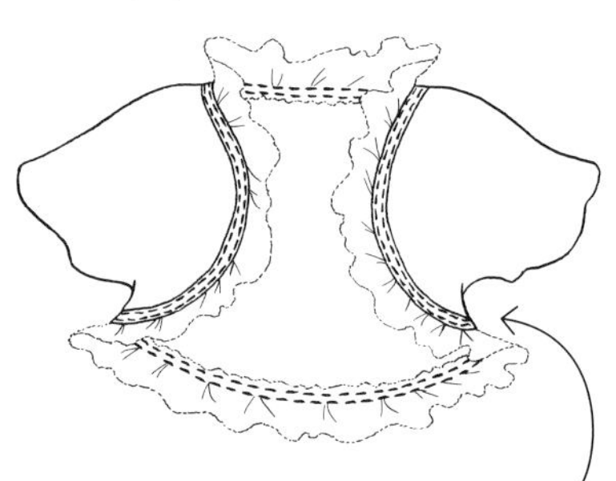

6. Trim any excess sweater threads that may be poking out from beneath the ribbon trim.

TOP 10 THINGS TO DO IN YOUR

Frilled and Fabulous

1. Wear white gloves.
2. Plant a rose garden.
3. Pick up a copy of *Tiffany's Table Manners for Teenagers* (no matter how old you are).
4. Attend a polo match.
5. Put your hair up in a bun.
6. Have a tea party in your front yard (make sure your dog attends, wearing her jacket as well).
7. Sip a mint julep.
8. Eat cucumber sandwiches for lunch.
9. Buy a fabulous hat.
10. Watch *Driving Miss Daisy*.

Frilled and Fabulous Pooch

WHAT YOU'LL NEED

- **Fingering-weight cashmere or wool sweater (or leftover material from the Frilled and Fabulous project)**
- **Choker necklace with adjustable length (measure your pooch's neck for the size)**
- **1 yard of ribbon, 2 inches wide**
- **1 yard of lace trim, 3 inches wide**
- **1 yard of ribbon, ½ inch wide**
- **6 inches of decorative ribbon**
- **Needle and thread and/or sewing machine**
- **Scissors**
- **Seamstress tape**
- **Straight pins**

Once you've made the Frilled and Fabulous sweater for yourself, you may have enough leftover sweater material for this quick and easy project—a matching sweater for your dearest little snuggle ball of fur, in this case Harley (although if your favorite pooch is a Great Dane, you may need a fresh sweater to cut up). This is an "oh so chic" project to have going on when you take your dog out for a walk on a cool spring evening.

DIRECTIONS

1. Using seamstress tape, measure your dog from neck to derriere, then around the middle.

2. Cut a rectangle in the dimensions of your dog's body.

3. Close the choker necklace to a width that fits comfortably around your dog's neck. Center it on one end of the rectangle and pin. Hand-sew about 3–4 inches of the necklace to the fabric. Hold the fabric tightly under the necklace, and loop your stitches through the necklace chains and sweater.

4. Fold down the fabric corners on the necklace end and secure with a few stitches.

5. Cut the fabric on the end opposite from the choker into a point or curve (or just leave a blunt rectangular shape).

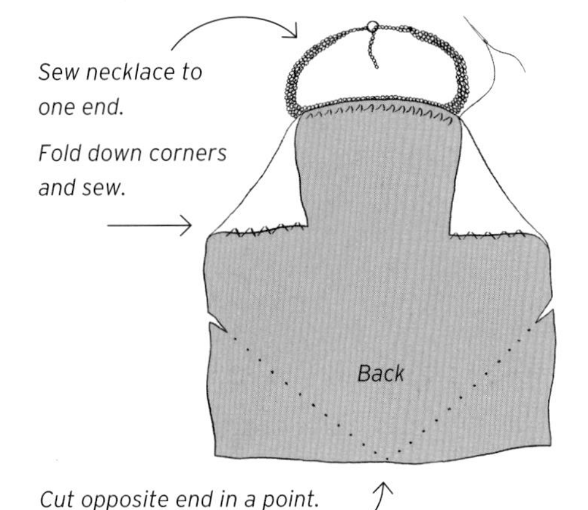

6. Sew the lace trim along the bottom edge, on the outside, with a loose straight stitch, bunching the lace as you sew.

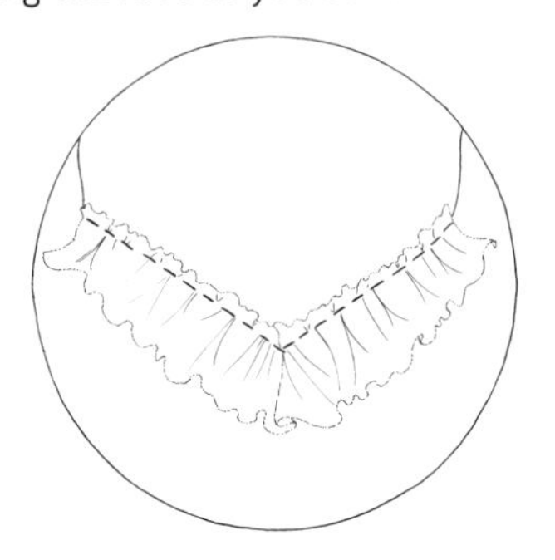

7. Sew the ½-inch ribbon on top of the bunched lace with a simple straight stitch.

8. Pin the decorative ribbon to the middle of the 2-inch ribbon and sew it down. Then sew the 2-inch ribbon across the middle of the dog sweater, leaving tails at each end to tie in a bow under the dog's belly.

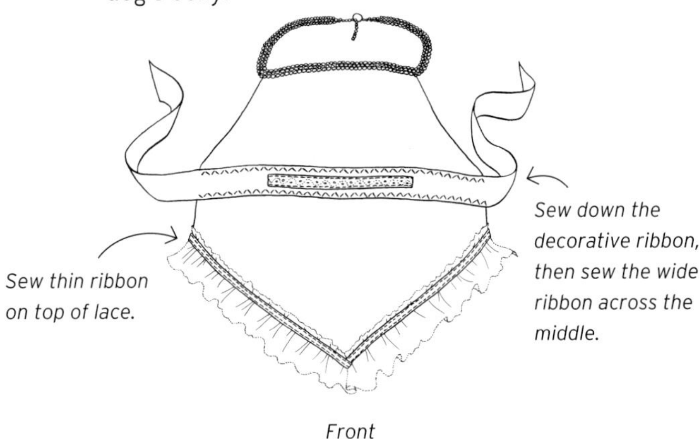

TOP 10 THINGS FOR YOUR DOG TO DO IN

Frilled and Fabulous Pooch

1. Eat a doggie treat from Sprinkles Cupcakes in Beverly Hills.
2. Roll around in the front yard.
3. Wear a heart pendant with your owner's name on it.
4. Drink water out of an antique teacup.
5. Chase around a cat named Minou.
6. Lounge on a brocade dog bed.
7. Chase around a blue jay.
8. Make friends with a squirrel.
9. Walk your owner around the neighborhood in her matching sweater.
10. Share a doggie treat with a friend.

Variation

If your pooch is more on the no-frills side, leave the lace off and simply finish the bottom with a neat hem or a tasseled fringe. Here's how to make a tasseled fringe:

1. Cut about ten 8-inch pieces of yarn or ribbon for each tassel.
2. Take one bunch of yarn or ribbon pieces. Fold the bunch in half and weave through the bottom of the sweater, ½ inch from the hem.
3. Pull ends through the loop as shown.

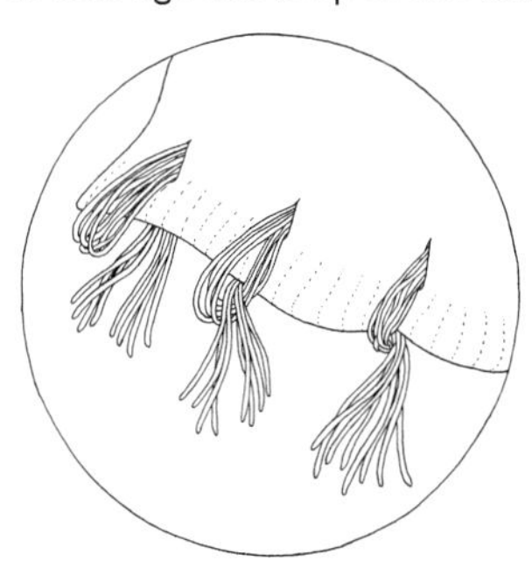

4. Repeat every couple of inches until the end of the hem.

turtleneck Purse

This purse was made using the neck of a sweater exactly like the one I used for Highland Lass (in a different color, on page 58). Can you believe I had two of these sweaters? I think they must have been on sale. Cindy, my best friend, has one in light blue that I may steal in the near future for another creation I have in mind. This is a quick project that doesn't take too many supplies, and is a great way to use every part of the sweater and some spare ribbon you may have lying around. Waste not, want not!

WHAT YOU'LL NEED

- **Wooden purse handle**
- **Worsted-weight wool turtleneck sweater (or at least the neck from one)**
- **Ribbon for wrapping purse (measure the circumference of the bottom of the purse and add an inch or two for good measure)**
- **Ruffled ribbon edging for bottom of purse (enough to stretch across bottom)**
- **20-inch of ribbon for tying on handle, ¼ inch wide**
- **4 medium grommets and grommet-setting tool**
- **Hammer**
- **4 scraps of heavy denim or canvas cloth**
- **12-inch leather cord**
- **Needle and thread or sewing machine**
- **4 silk flowers (optional)**

DIRECTIONS

1. Cut the neck off your sweater. Cut straight across the bottom so it maintains a rectangular shape.

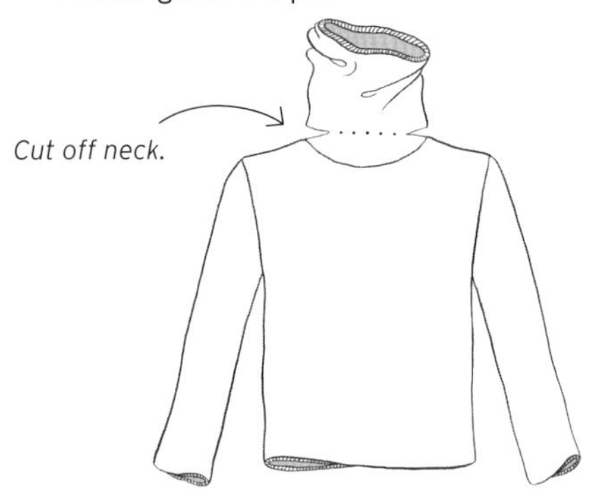

2. Soak the turtleneck in warm water so it shrinks a little. Let it air-dry.

3. Turn the neck inside out. Sew the raw ends of the tube closed with a straight stitch going across; this will be the bottom of the purse. Turn right-side out.

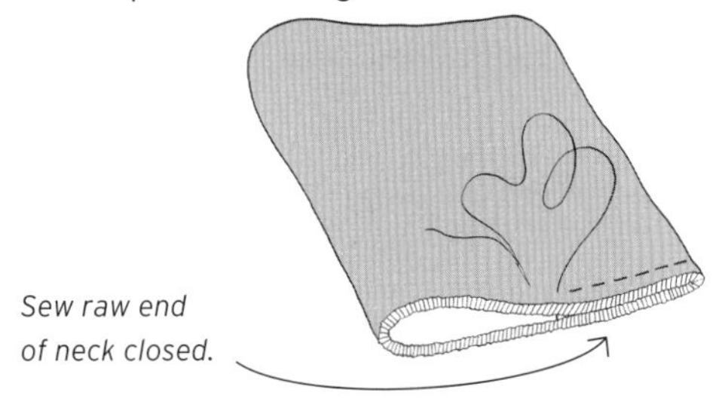

4. If you are using more than one kind of ribbon, sew the ribbons together lengthwise to create a wide strip. In the project shown, I used three different kinds of ribbon sewn together.

5. Pin your ribbon strip around the bottom of your purse, making sure the strip overhangs the purse bottom by about 1 inch. Hand-sew the strip down along the top edge only. Fold under the overlapping ribbon and use a straight stitch to close the circle.

6. Bring the edges of your ribbon strip underneath the purse so they meet. Take your ruffled ribbon and sandwich it between the edges of the strip. Sew a straight stitch across the bottom, creating another bottom seam and securing the "sandwich." The ruffled ribbon edging should protrude out the bottom.

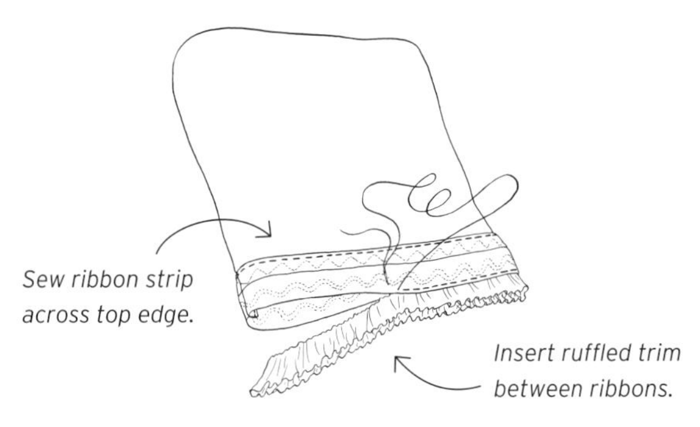

7. Get your purse handle and mark where the holes should fall on the purse. Add two grommets on each side of the purse (where the holes should be), backing all four grommets with a denim scrap to reinforce them.

8. Cut your leather cord in half, creating two 6-inch pieces. Pull one piece through the grommets and purse handle on one side, knotting the ends enough so that the leather cord does not pull through the grommet. Repeat with the other cord on the other side.

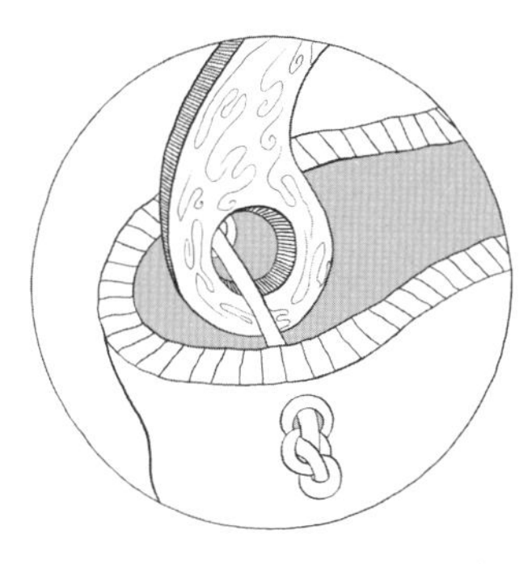

9. Cut your 20-inch piece of ribbon in half. Run each piece through one side of the holes and handle, over the leather, and make a bow to cover the knotted cord. Sew the bows in place.

10. Sew a silk flower to the middle of each of the four bows (optional).

TOP 10 THINGS TO DO WHILE CARRYING YOUR Turtleneck Purse

1. Listen to Sting's *The Dream of the Blue Turtles*.
2. Wear tortoiseshell hair clip (faux).
3. Adopt a pet turtle.
4. Crawl into your shell for a day of quality alone time.
5. Strum your guitar with a plastic tortoiseshell pick.
6. Eat a turtle—the chocolate-caramel kind of course!
7. Relax and take things *sloooow*.
8. Visit the Galapagos Islands and see the giant tortoises.
9. Read "The Hare and the Tortoise" in *Aesop's Fables*.
10. Donate to a tortoise conservation fund.

tango top

WHAT YOU'LL NEED

- **Stretchy fingering-weight knit sweater in wool, cashmere, silk, or any synthetic blend**
- **Scarf in any silky material (silk or polyester), 20 × 30 inches**
- **Needle and thread and/or sewing machine**
- **Scissors**
- **Seamstress tape or ruler**
- **Fabric pencil**
- **Brooch or snap for closure**

This playful top gives off a sexy, fun vibe. Wearing it will awaken your adventurous spirit and make you crave travel to foreign lands to watch bullfights, sip delicious cocktails, and eat papaya, mango, and passion fruit. This top almost reminds me of a bullfighter's short jacket with slightly flared sleeves. !Olé!

DIRECTIONS

1. Put the sweater on. Measure 4 inches up from your belly button and make a mark. Make two more marks where your elbows fall in the sleeves. Take the sweater off. Cut off the bottom of the sweater, straight across, at your mark. Cut the sleeves straight across using your marks as guides.

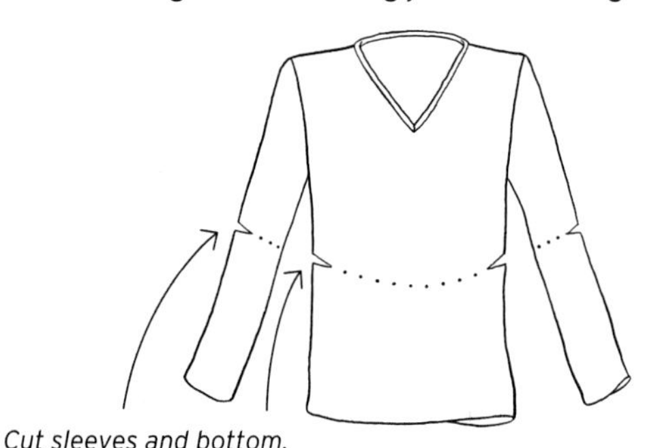

Cut sleeves and bottom.

2. Lay the sweater face up. Cut a slightly curved "X" shape out of the front only, going up either side of the neckline and around the back of the neck. The middle of the "X" should be just under your bustline.

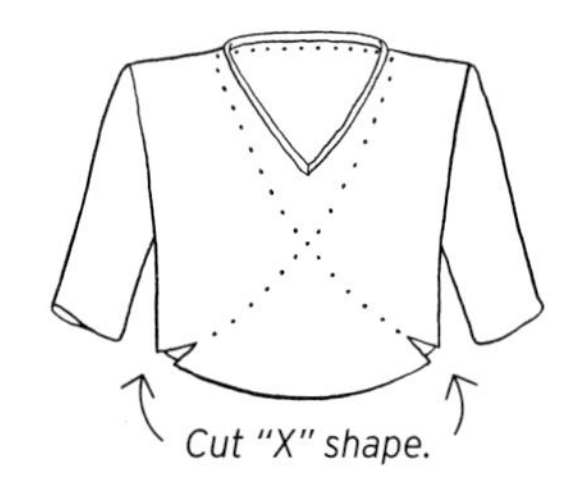

Cut "X" shape.

3. Put the sweater back on and stretch it out, pulling together the two bottoms of the "V" to make sure they can meet and overlap slightly.

4. Take the scarf and cut 4 inches from each long side. You will be left with two strips measuring 4 × 30 inches, and a middle strip that measures 12 × 30 inches.

5. Take the two 4-inch strips and lay them end to end. Sew them together, creating a very long strip measuring 4 × 60 inches. Then fold your strip in half lengthwise, so that it is 2 × 60 inches. Sew together the two edges, making a long seam.

6. You're going to sew the strip around the bottom of the sweater, using a face-to-face seam (see page 29). Pin the sewn edge of the strip around the bottom of the sweater, pleating the fabric as you pin it down.

7. Sew down the ruffled strip.

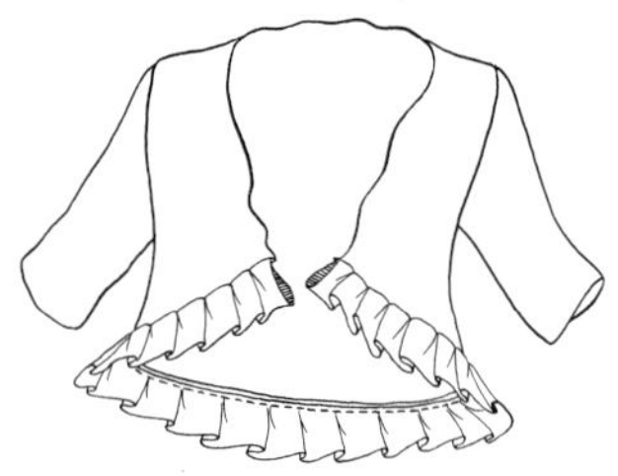

8. Now you're going to trim the sleeves. First, stretch the sleeves out a little.

9. Get that middle strip of the scarf—the 12 × 30-inch piece—and cut it in half lengthwise so you have two strips, each 6 × 30 inches. Now fold each piece widthwise, so that it measures 6 × 15 inches. Sew one end shut.

10. Pin the open end of the trim to the bottom of each sleeve, then sew down with a face-to-face seam, stretching the knit as you sew. Sew the ends of the trim together with a seam on the inside.

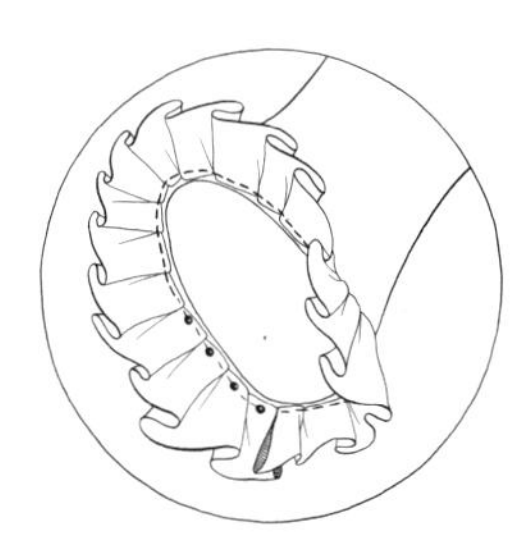

11. To wear, pin the "V" shut with a brooch or add a snap for closure.

TOP 10 THINGS TO DO IN YOUR

tango top

1. Go on a hot date and have a giant strawberry margarita.
2. Find out more about Frida Kahlo.
3. Learn to tango.
4. Have a passionate discussion.
5. Travel to Argentina.
6. Wear red pants.
7. Get a palm reading.
8. Watch *The Red Violin*.
9. Rock out to Shakira.
10. Ride an elephant.

Highland Lass

Vivienne Westwood is one of my favorite designers, and her dirty, ripped clothing was on the cutting edge in the 1970s, introducing punk into the vocabulary of modern style. She drew inspiration from what was happening on the streets of London as well as from historic British shapes and patterns. This sweater is inspired by her awesome style.

WHAT YOU'LL NEED

- **Fitted worsted-weight crew or V-neck sweater**
- **Pleated plaid skirt**
- **2 yards of ribbon, ¼ inch wide**
- **4 yards of ribbon in contrasting color, ¼ inch wide**
- **2 buttons (add one more if you want to make the pocket)**
- **Needle and thread**
- **Safety pins**
- **Fabric pencil**
- **Scissors**
- **Fray Check**
- **Embroidery thread (optional, for the pocket)**
- **Iron (optional)**

DIRECTIONS

1. Put the sweater on. With a fabric pencil, mark how low you want your scoop neck to go. Also mark where your elbows fall in the sleeves. Take the sweater off.

2. Cut the front of your sweater straight up the middle, creating a cardigan. Cut across the sleeves where you marked them.

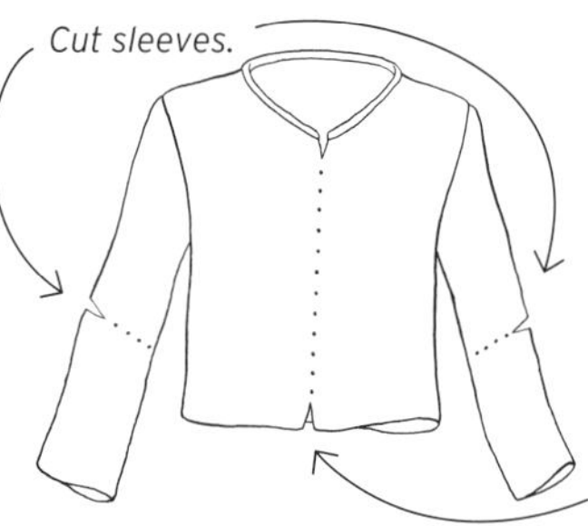

3. Cut a scoop neck on one side only, using your mark as a guide, going from the center to just before the shoulder seam. (Don't cut the shoulder seam, or the neckline will stretch too wide to maintain its size.) Leave the back uncut.

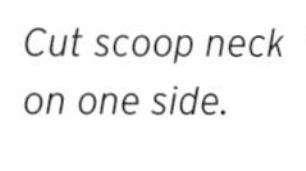

4. Take the cutout neckline piece and lay it over the other side, using it as a stencil to cut that side. This ensures that both sides are symmetrical.

5. Sew a straight stitch along the newly cut neckline to keep it from stretching out.

6. Fold over the top corner of each side of the neckline and sew down a button so the folded corners stay put.

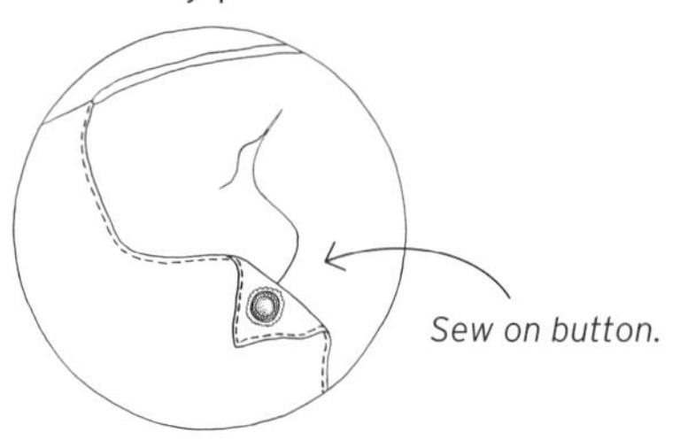

7. Attach the safety pin to one end of a ribbon. Use the pin to weave the ribbon through the sweater, up one side of the center opening, around the neckline, and down the other side of the center. Keep your weave very loose to avoid bunching up the sweater. Knot the ribbon at the starting and ending points on the inside to secure. Cut off the extra ribbon.

8. Repeat with the second color ribbon, weaving it parallel to the first and about ½ inch away.

9. Get the plaid skirt. Cut a strip of fabric from the bottom about 6 inches wide. Cut that strip in half to form two lengths. You're going to use this fabric to trim the sleeves.

10. Stretch one sleeve wide. Pin the hemmed edge of the plaid fabric around the bottom

TOP 10 THINGS TO DO IN Highland Lass

1 Read a Sherlock Holmes story.

2 Google that exchange student you had a crush on in high school.

3 Listen to the Sex Pistols.

4 Walk your neighbor's greyhound.

5 Brainstorm and design a coat of arms for yourself.

6 Buy a candle snuff.

7 Drink Earl Grey tea with milk and sugar, and eat shortbread cookies.

8 Write a letter and seal it with a wax seal.

9 Watch old episodes of *Ab Fab*.

10 Make a bacon sarnie.

of the sleeve on the inside, keeping the pleats in place. Sew with an old-overlapping-new seam, using a straight stitch, stretching the knit sleeve as you go. Sew the open edges together with a seam on the inside.

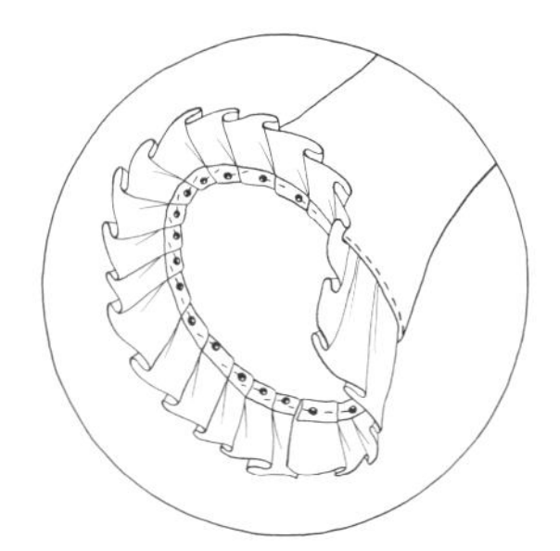

11. Fray the bottom edge of the plaid fabric by pulling on the threads that run lengthwise, then add Fray Check.

12. Repeat steps 10–11 for the other sleeve.

13. Get the extra ribbon. Attach the safety pin to one end and weave around each sleeve as shown in the photo. Tie each ribbon in a bow to finish.

Optional pocket

14. If there is extra plaid fabric, use it to add a pocket. Cut out a square of fabric. Hem the raw edges by folding them under ¼ inch all around and ironing them down, and then sew a button in the middle. Pin the square where you want your pocket. Sew the pocket to the sweater using embroidery thread.

Granny Bolero

WHAT YOU'LL NEED

- **Embroidered granny cardigan in any knit (don't worry if it's too big)**
- **Needle and thread**
- **Sewing machine**
- **Fabric pencil (or just an ordinary pencil)**
- **Scissors**
- **Straight pins**

I see these cardigans at thrift shops all the time. They sit there on the rack for ages; no one will touch them because they are so out of style. What I think is so adorable about them are the embroidered flowers that grace both sides of the button-down front. They're so sweet and lovely—and quite a bit of work if you were to embroider them yourself. I get oodles and oodles of compliments on this little number, well worth the work.

DIRECTIONS

1. Put the sweater on. Mark where you would like your bolero bottom to fall. Also mark where your elbows hit the sleeves. Take the sweater off.

2. Cut across the bottom *2 inches below* your mark, straight across. (Save the fabric you cut off for later.) Cut each sleeve right below your mark; cut on a diagonal, starting lower on the inner seam and slanting up.

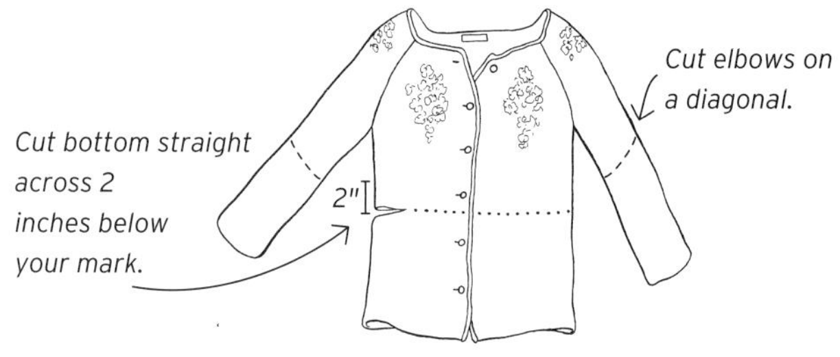

3. Button the last two buttons and figure out how fitted you would like the bottom of the sweater to be. Measure the excess. This is how much you need to take the sweater in.

4. Open the sweater and lay it flat, with the inside of the back facing up. Measure halfway between one of the side seams and the midpoint of the back, and make a $\frac{1}{4}$-inch pleat as shown. Pin it down. Repeat from other side seam.

5. Sew each pleat, starting at the bottom and going up, until it forms a triangle-shaped flap about 5 inches long. This is called a dart.

Sew two darts into the back.

6. Now turn to the front of the sweater. Starting 4 inches from one side seam, make $\frac{1}{8}$-inch pleats along the bottom of the sweater, continuing around to the back until you reach the dart, pinning them as you go. Sew a straight line across, from the first pleat to the dart, $1\frac{1}{2}$ inches up from the bottom of the sweater. Repeat on the other side.

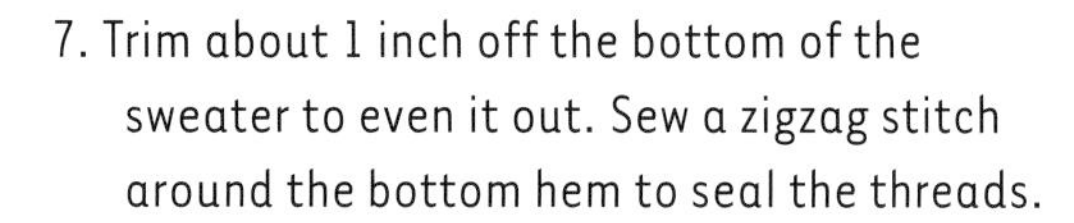

7. Trim about 1 inch off the bottom of the sweater to even it out. Sew a zigzag stitch around the bottom hem to seal the threads.

8. Take the extra fabric you cut off the bottom in step 2. Cut it into two strips, each 4 inches wide and as long as possible.

9. You're going to attach a strip around the inside of each sleeve end. Get your first strip and, leaving $\frac{1}{4}$ inch extra at the end, use a zigzag stitch to sew it around one sleeve, pleating the strip slightly as you go. When you're done, trim off the excess. Sew the cutoff edges of the strip closed with a seam on the inside.

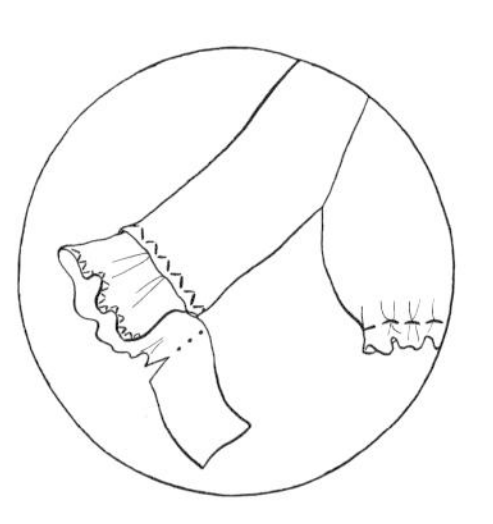

10. Repeat step 9 for the other sleeve.

TOP 10 THINGS TO DO IN YOUR

Granny Bolero

1. Bring your neighbor flowers.
2. Call your grandma.
3. Prune a rosebush.
4. Bake oatmeal raisin cookies.
5. Wear comfortable shoes.
6. Learn to knit.
7. Wear *Youth Dew*, by Estée Lauder.
8. Find a photo of your grandma at the same age you are now.
9. Make a family collage.
10. Buy funky reading glasses and use them as an accessory.

tank tops and t-shirts

WHAT YOU'LL NEED

- **Black tank top**
- **2 ½ feet of lace, 5 inches wide**
- **2 feet of velvet ribbon, 1 ½ inches wide**
- **Needle and thread**
- **Hot glue gun (optional)**

Naughty See's Candy Lady

One thing I love about my neighborhood is that there is a See's Candies store right around the corner. If you've ever been in one, you probably know that they always give you a sample when you walk in the door; their Scotch Kisses and Toffee-ettes rock my lazy Saturday evenings. My favorite thing is the awesome white uniform with a black bow that the See's ladies wear, a throwback to the '50s when everyone in the food service industry sported a uniform—so old-fashioned and proper. This is my version, for a night on the town perhaps, or a date to a drive-in movie.

DIRECTIONS

1. Lay your lace on the front of the tank top in a tight "U" shape, with both ends hanging over the neckline and the two sides slightly overlapping. Fold the top edges over the neckline. Make a straight stitch across the 10-inch span, along the neckline seam, to secure.

Overlap lace and sew it along the neckline

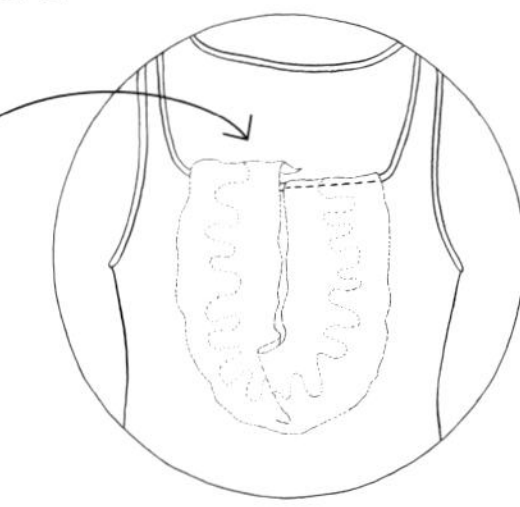

2. Make a pleat every 2 inches on each side of the "U" and one in the middle. Sew down the pleated points. Make sure that no large black areas are showing underneath the lace.

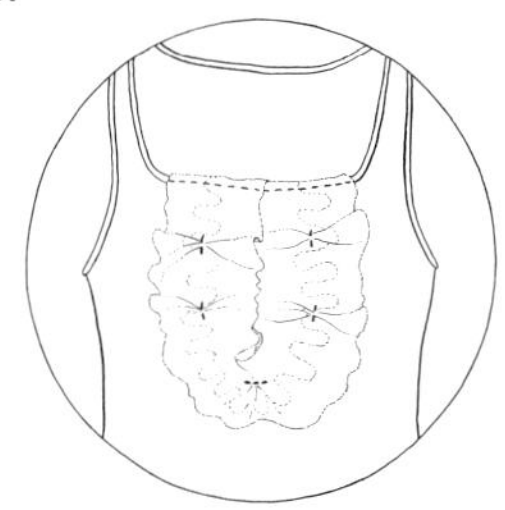

3. Tie the ribbon in a bow. Pin so that it is centered on the neckline, as shown, and sew or glue down to secure.

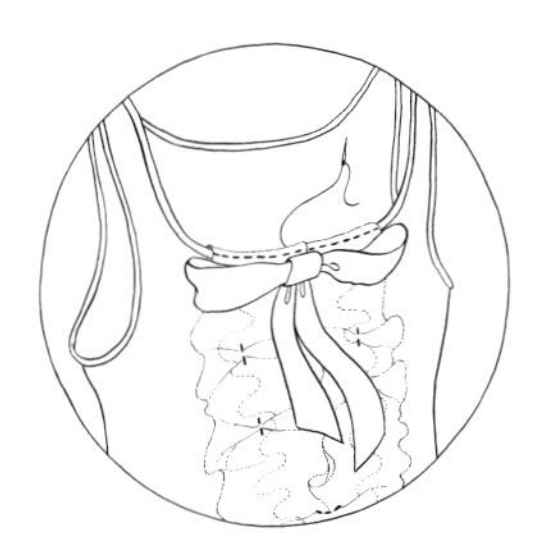

TOP 10 THINGS TO DO WHILE WEARING

Naughty See's Candy Lady

1 Pass out butterscotch kisses to cute boys at a concert.

2 Go to See's Candies and get free samples.

3 Wear fishnets and a short skirt and clean your house with a red feather duster.

4 Paint your nails white with black tips.

5 Tie a ribbon with a little brooch around your neck.

6 Wear a garter.

7 Order a T-bone steak at Mastro's in Beverly Hills.

8 Host a goth party.

9 Make coiled black licorice into matching jewelry.

10 Cut yourself some bangs.

Variation

Use old underwear or lingerie instead of store-bought lace. (How about the lacy ones your ex bought you that you wore only once?) The key here is to cut out the crotch and trim the lacy parts into a collar shape—you don't want to be caught with your underwear hanging around your neck!

WHAT YOU'LL NEED

- Tank top
- 8 inches of satin ribbon, 1 inch wide (navy blue used here)
- 16 inches of velvet ribbon, ½ inch wide (brown used here)
- 16 inches of cream lace, ½ inch wide
- 3 buttons
- Scissors
- Needle and thread
- Sewing machine (optional)
- Straight pins

Buttoned Up

I really don't miss being in school—frankly, I could never relax. Don't get me wrong, I did well, but I'm glad I no longer have to deal with term papers, deadlines, and finals. Whew! But I do miss those preppy clothes. Real leather buttons and soft velvet ribbon trim make "Buttoned Up" the perfect collegiate top.

DIRECTIONS

1. Cut the velvet ribbon in half lengthwise so you have two pieces of 8-inch ribbon. Line up the satin ribbon with one piece of the velvet ribbon on either side, as shown in the photo, the edges of the brown ribbon overlapping the navy ribbon slightly. Pin together.

2. Sew the three pieces of ribbon together using a straight stitch on either side of the middle ribbon.

3. Sew lace in a "U" shape around the outside edge of the ribbons.

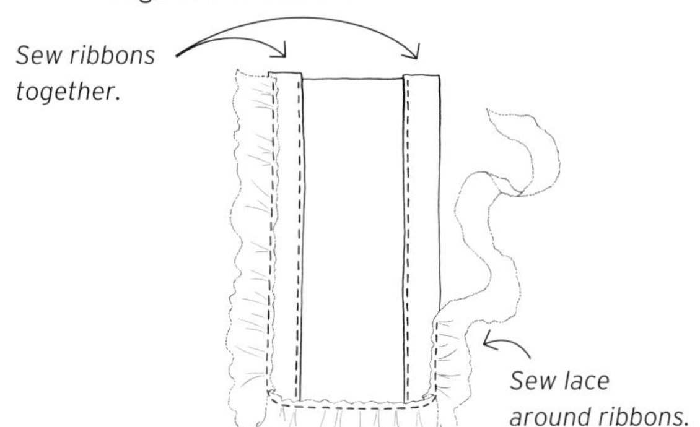

4. Get your tank top. Fold the top ½ inch of the lace-and-ribbon piece over the center of the tank top neckline and pin down.

5. Sew the decorative piece to the tank top along the top. Also sew a seam going around the piece, between the lace and the velvet ribbon, using a straight stitch.

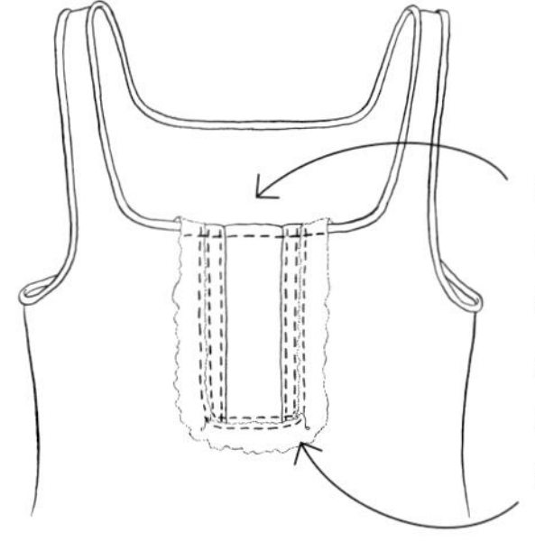

TOP 10 THINGS TO DO WHILE WEARING Buttoned Up

1 Wear your old cheerleading skirt.

2 Go to the library and check out a book you've always wanted to read.

3 Find that blazer you thought you lost.

4 Wear glasses instead of contacts.

5 Enroll in a class to help you with your money management skills.

6 Wear knee-high socks.

7 Call your high school boyfriend.

8 Watch *Dead Poet's Society*.

9 Read your yearbook.

10 Pass notes with a coworker.

6. Sew three buttons down the center of the satin ribbon.

Variation

Cut a collar off another shirt and sew it to a tank top; then add buttons going down the middle of the front.

Lacy/DC

This was originally a stretchy black, long-sleeved shirt—another one of those work numbers that gets really boring after a while. My friend Cindy gave me this shirt after she quit her day job and decided to move to Italy to enjoy the vino and prosciutto. I always prefer cardigans over pullovers because they're easier to take on and off, so I slit the shirt up the middle and turned it into this subversive little number.

WHAT YOU'LL NEED

- **Snug-fitting long-sleeved lightweight stretchy crewneck shirt in an acrylic, wool, polyester, or Lycra blend**
- **2 ½-feet of pleated ribbon, 1 inch wide**
- **Scissors**
- **Large snap**
- **Large button**
- **Fabric pencil**
- **Needle and thread**
- **Sewing machine (optional)**

DIRECTIONS

1. Put the shirt on and mark where you want the bottom of the bolero to fall. Also mark where your elbows hit the sleeves. Take the shirt off.

2. Cut straight across the bottom at your mark. Cut the sleeves at your marks as well.

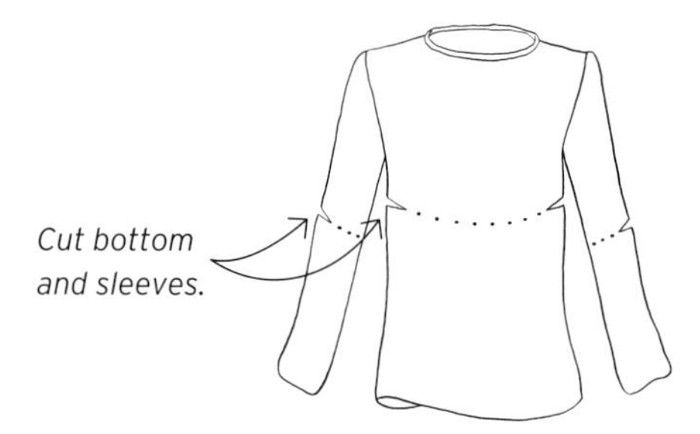

3. Cut the shirt straight down the middle, creating a cardigan.

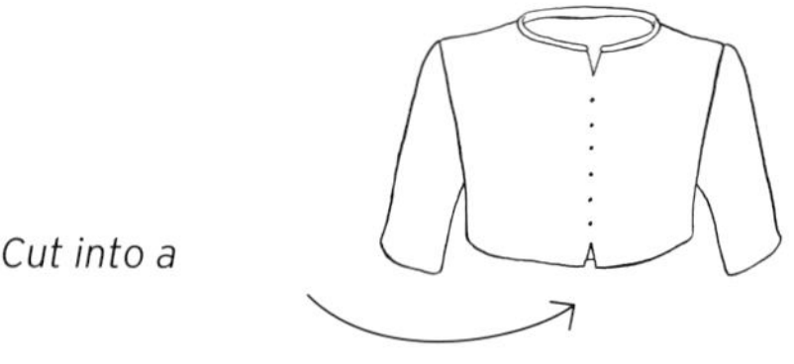

4. Starting an inch down from the collar, make a 1-inch horizontal cut, then swoop in and down with the scissors to create a bolero shape on one side, ending at the seam.

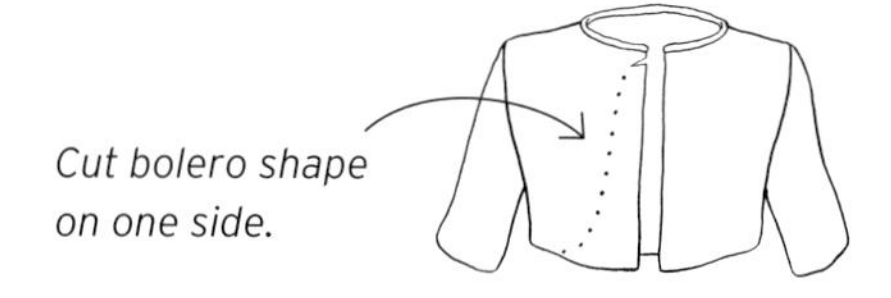

5. Take the cutout piece and lay it on the other side of the shirt. Use it as a stencil to cut out the same shape.

6. Hem the raw edges of the sleeves by hand or using a zigzag stitch.

7. Hem the raw shirt edge as well, by hand or using a zigzag stitch.

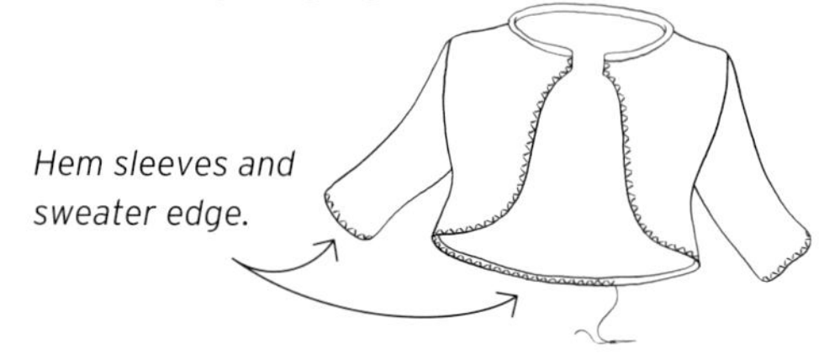

8. If you don't like the shape of the neckline, cut it to your desired shape.

9. Sew the ribbon around the neckline, either by hand or machine, using a straight stitch. Leave an extra inch of ribbon at each end to be turned under and sewed down for a neat finish.

10. Hand-sew a snap to either side of the collar so that it snaps shut in the middle.

11. Sew the button over the spot where the snap sits, to hide your stitches.

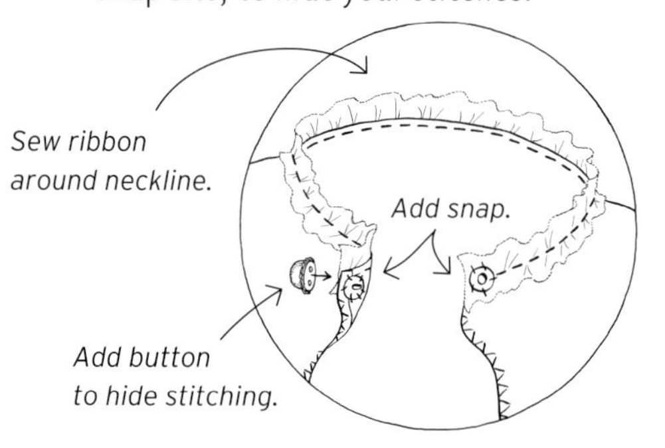

Variation

Appliqué pieces of fabric or lace on the arms, chest, and/or back.

TOP 10 THINGS TO DO IN Lacy/DC

1. Start your own garage band.
2. Play air guitar on your bed.
3. Find your old AC/DC tapes.
4. Buy some black satin sheets.
5. Connect with your favorite bands on MySpace.
6. Cut the fingertips off your black gloves and glue jewels to them.
7. Paint your nails black.
8. Apply for a job as a roadie for a death metal band.
9. Just say "no" to everything and everyone.
10. Rip holes in your tights.

Laced with Charm

Tank tops are one of those things that everyone's got lying around. They are the perfect blank canvas for a makeover. This project is easy as pie and takes less than half an hour to complete. It's so feminine and sweet; you'll love being a girly girl in this.

WHAT YOU'LL NEED

- **Tank top**
- **2 feet of satin ribbon, ½ inch wide (for the neckline)**
- **2 yards of satin ribbon, 1 inch wide (for the sides)**
- **1 yard of lace, 5 ½ inches wide**
- **Pinking shears**
- **Small pointed nail scissors or embroidery scissors**
- **Safety pins**
- **Needle and thread**
- **Fabric pencil (optional)**
- **1 foot of ribbon, 1 inch wide (optional: for the heart)**

DIRECTIONS

1. Taking the end of the tiny scissors, make small holes all around the neckline at even intervals by inserting the point between the fibers. Try not to break threads—sometimes doing so is inevitable, but just make sure the holes stay as small as possible.

2. Attach a safety pin to one end of your ½-inch ribbon. Starting below the shoulder, weave the ribbon through the holes, going all around. To finish, make a bow. Secure the bow to the tank top with a few stitches.

Side lacing

3. Using the same technique as in step 1, make two parallel rows of small holes, moving down each side seam. The rows should run parallel to each other, one going down either side of the seam, spaced ½ inch apart and starting ½ inch down from the arm hole. Do this on each side.

4. Get your 1-inch ribbon and cut it into two equal lengths. Attach a safety pin to each end of one of the pieces and lace it back and forth through the holes, as if you're lacing a shoe. Tie a knot at the bottom. Repeat for the other side.

Sleeves

5. Cut two pieces of the lace, each about 11 inches long. Pin each to an armhole, along the inside. Pleat the lace if you wish to create a lift at the top of the shoulder seam. Notice that the lace does not go all the way around the armhole; it's more like a cap sleeve.

6. Turn the tank top inside out and hand-sew the lace along each armhole seam, as pinned.

Bottom (optional)

7. Measure the bottom of the tank top stretched. Cut a piece of lace that's just a bit longer than half its circumference. Then cut the piece in half lengthwise.

8. Pin one piece of the lace along the bottom of the front, on the inside. Pin the other piece to the back. Sew down.

Heart decoration (optional)

9. Sketch a heart shape onto your tank top with fabric pencil, then use your tiny scissors to poke holes through the tank top in a heart shape.

TOP 10 THINGS TO DO WHILE WEARING

Laced with Charm

1 Ride a carousel.
2 Go to the pier and get cotton candy.
3 Make a mini–Laced with Charm shirt for a friend's baby.
4 Go to charm school.
5 See *Pretty in Pink* starring Molly Ringwald.
6 Buy yourself a charm bracelet.
7 Glue pink Swarovski crystals to your cell phone.
8 Eat a big bowl of Lucky Charms.
9 Buy flowers for your prince charming.
10 Wear bright pink lip gloss.

10. Weave ribbon through the holes, ending with both ends of the ribbon on the inside of the tank top. Tie in a knot.

Variation

Instead of using lace for the sleeves, use wide ribbon (2–3 inches wide) or strips of raw fabric. The lacing on the neckline and the sides can also be done with strips of fabric, lengths of lace, or decorative rope.

Fräulein Über-Vamp

WHAT YOU'LL NEED

- **Rayon-blend or spandex-blend shirt (any blend that stretches will do)**
- **¼ yard of plaid Thai silk**
- **Scissors**
- **Straight pins**
- **Fray Check**
- **Needle and thread or sewing machine**
- **Seamstress tape**

One of my favorite movies of all time is The Sound of Music. *(It's really an American thing to love this movie—when I was in Austria a couple of years ago no one had seen it!) I love the scene where Maria makes play clothes for the children out of the brocade curtains, then takes them out for a day on the town. She must have been the fastest sewer in the world to make seven outfits in one night—and have had ESP to know their measurements. I also love the flattering square-neckline dress that Maria wears in the film—a traditional Alpine cut. Here is my version of the square neckline that I so dearly love on her.*

DIRECTIONS

1. Rip a strip from the Thai silk that's 2 inches wide by 36 inches. Rip two more strips, each 2 inches wide by 18 inches long. Iron the strips to make sure the threads are straight (they might pucker with the ripping motion).

2. Apply Fray Check to the raw edges on each strip. Let dry.

3. If the neckline of your shirt is not the desired shape, put it on and mark where you want the neckline to fall. Do the same for the sleeves. Take the shirt off, and cut the neckline and sleeves using your marks as guides.

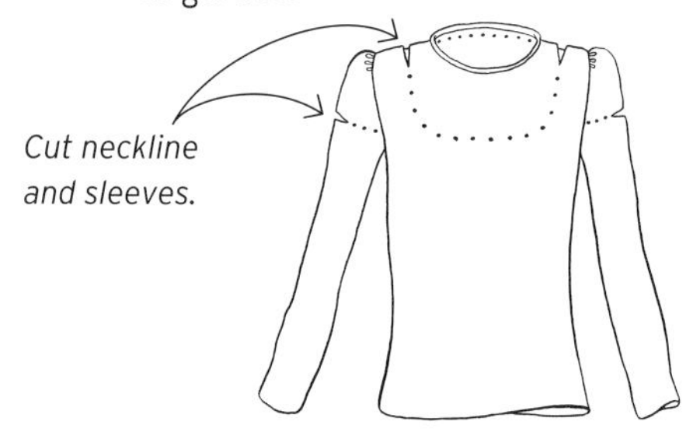
Cut neckline and sleeves.

4. Get the 2 × 36 inch strip of silk. Fold it in half to find the center, then pin that point to the center of your neckline on the outside. Pin the rest of the strip around the neckline, bunching as you go to make the ruffle. End your ruffle at each shoulder seam.

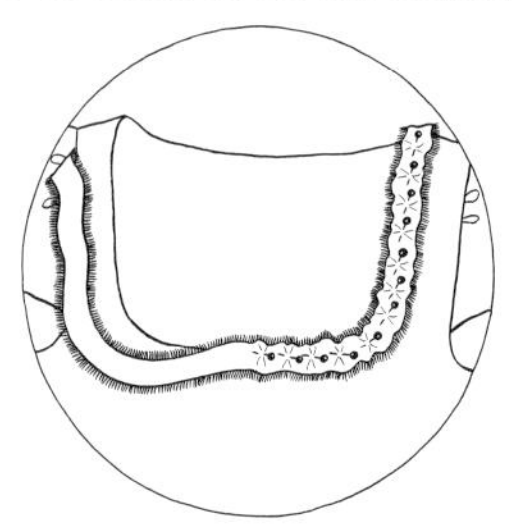

5. Zigzag stitch or hand-sew the silk to the neckline, starting at one shoulder seam and sewing around to the other.

6. Get one of the 2 × 18 inch strips. Pin it around one sleeve, bunching as you go so that it matches the ruffle on the neckline. The strip can go all the way around the sleeve, or, if you want a cap sleeve, end where the sleeve meets the body of the shirt by turning under the silk and ending your stitch there. Sew with a straight stitch right in the center of the silk strip to the edge of the sleeve.

7. Repeat step 6 for the other sleeve.

Variation

Instead of sewing a ruffle around the neckline, sew parallel ruffles in contrasting fabrics down the center of the shirt to go for a '70s prom tuxedo shirt look.

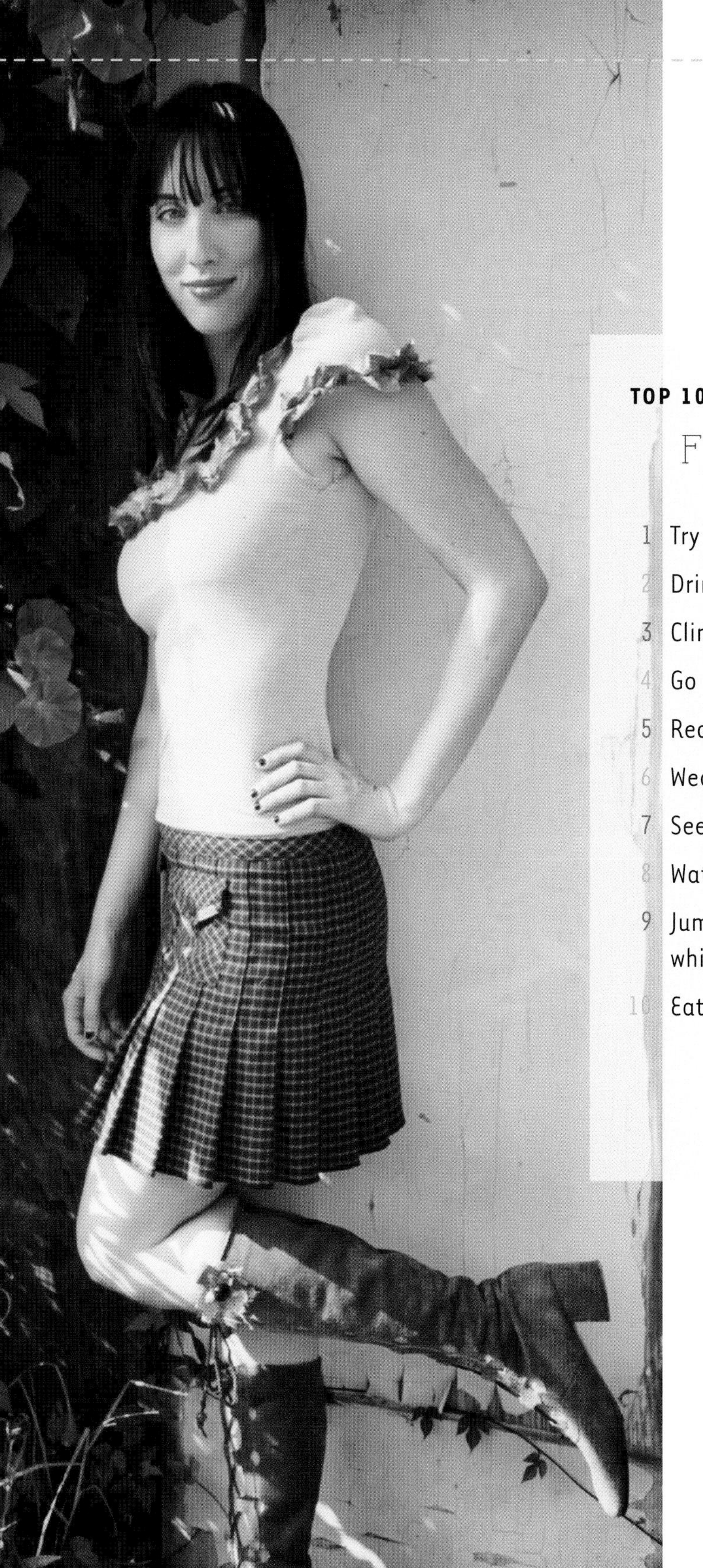

TOP 10 THINGS TO DO WHILE WEARING

Fräulein Über-Vamp

1. Try yodeling.
2. Drink whole milk straight out of a glass bottle.
3. Climb a mountain.
4. Go on a picnic with all of your siblings.
5. Read *The Story of the Trapp Family Singers*.
6. Wear braids and ribbons in your hair.
7. See a puppet show.
8. Watch *The Sound of Music*.
9. Jump up and down the steps of a public building while singing scales.
10. Eat Wiener schnitzel.

dresses and skirts

WHAT YOU'LL NEED

- Skirt in a nonstretch fabric such as khaki, denim, or wool (no Lycra blends or stretchy spandex numbers)
- Lace or ruffle trim a couple of inches longer than the bottom hem (if there's a slit, include that length in your measurements)
- Ribbon the same length as your ruffle trim
- Needle and thread (buy thread in colors that match your trims)
- Straight pins

Ruffled Around the Edges

This is a really simple way to add an innocent yet flirtatious edge to any plain-Jane office skirt, whether it has a slit or not. My friend Tina gave me this skirt because, though she really liked it, she could never find a place to wear it. It was a bit too dressy for work but not quite right for a night out. I added a little lace and ribbon and find it great for a lunch date at the Ivy or a trip to the Getty Villa in Malibu.

DIRECTIONS

1. Starting at the most inconspicuous place on the skirt, pin the lace or ruffle trim around the bottom edge on the inside so that it is just peeping out. Turn your skirt inside out and hand-sew down the trim, using thread the same color as the trim and making sure the stitching does not show on the front of the skirt.

2. Turn the skirt right-side out. Starting at the same place you began the ruffle, pin the ribbon trim around on the outside, ¼ inch from the edge of the skirt. Sew it down, using thread the same color as the ribbon, so you can sew through the ribbon without the thread showing.

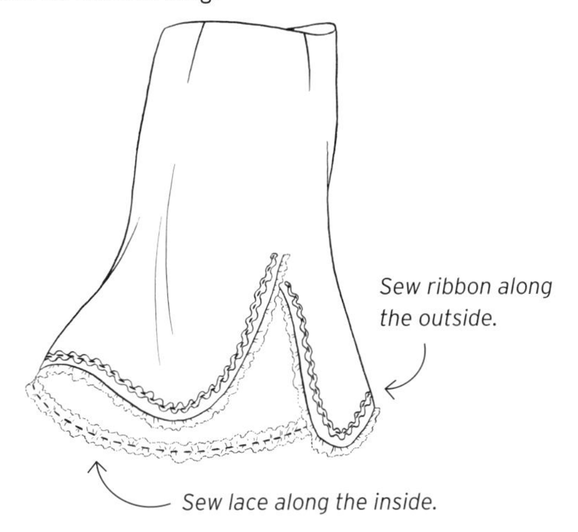

TOP 10 THINGS TO DO WHILE WEARING

Ruffled Around the Edges

1. Get a tattoo of a flower.
2. Wear ruffled underwear.
3. Ride a lavender scooter around your block.
4. Bat your eyelashes demurely.
5. Buy yourself an antique ring.
6. Flirt with everyone for a day.
7. Talk to the garden fairies.
8. Find your nearest garden store and buy yourself a new flowering plant.
9. Listen to Carla Bruni's *Quelqu'un M'a Dit*.
10. Treat yourself to a French manicure.

WHAT YOU'LL NEED

- Nonstretchy black dress in cotton or wool
- 3 yards of lace trim, ½ inch wide
- Needle and thread
- Straight pins
- Chain necklace that is at least long enough to extend from one side seam to the other at your waist
- Wire cutters

Mademoiselle Coco

I am a big fan of the little black dress. I got this one a long, long time ago at a second-hand store but quickly became a bit bored with it. After inheriting a huge stash of costume jewelry, I glitzed it up with a chain across the front and lace around the hems. Voilà! Coco Chanel would be so proud.

DIRECTIONS

1. Pin the lace along the inside seams of the neckline, arms, and hem so that the lace is poking out the front. Start the lace in the back of the dress at each opening so the finishing overlaps (about ½-inch overlap is enough) are in inconspicuous places. Hand-sew the lace down, making sure the thread does not show on the outside of the dress by just catching the bottom threads on the inside lining of the dress.

2. Take the chain and pin it across the front of the dress on the waistline seam.

3. Hand-sew the chain to the front of the dress, starting at the side seam, running the thread through from the inside of the dress and catching the chain links on the outside. Finish connecting your chain at the opposite side seam.

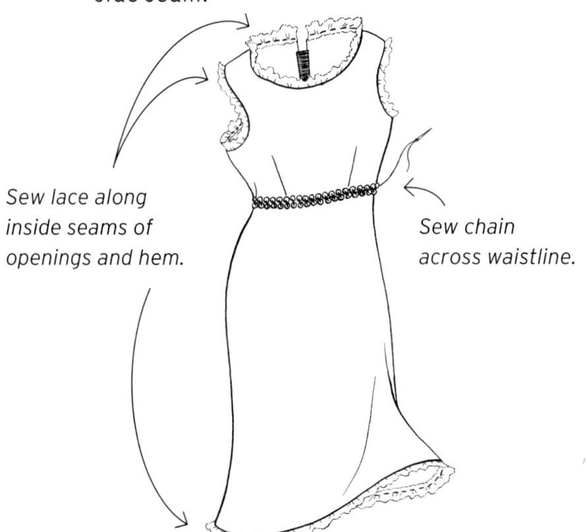

4. When you're done, trim off any excess chain links with wire cutters.

Variation

Switch the trims—use chain to trim the neck, sleeves, and hem, and sew the lace along the waistline seam. Or, add all elements to all four areas.

TOP 10 THINGS TO DO WHILE WEARING

Mademoiselle Coco

1. Call your boyfriend *mon amour* and look dramatically into his eyes while pouting.
2. Eat a fresh baguette with Nutella spread all over it.
3. Learn French.
4. Ask your mom for all the fake pearls she no longer wears and wear them all at once.
5. Wear Chanel No 5.
6. Go to a café alone and write a love letter while sipping café au lait.
7. Buy a ticket to Paris.
8. Research the life of Coco Chanel.
9. Wear your favorite lace panties.
10. Eat lunch out with your best friend.

WHAT YOU'LL NEED

- Piece of brocade fabric, 1 × 2½ feet
- 2 yards of ribbon, 1 ½ inches wide
- Needle and thread
- Scissors
- Iron and ironing board

Shabby Chic

I love brocade . . . in small doses. I must admit, I have a brocade blazer that I used to wear all the time in high school. These days, though, I find that a little goes a long way. Here, I took an upholstery sample I found in the attic and sewed it to a couple pieces of ribbon for a brocade belt that adds a bit of richness to any dress.

DIRECTIONS

1. Lay the brocade right-side up and fold it lengthwise as shown. The two raw edges should meet in the middle and overlap slightly. (The cummerbund will be inside out at this point.) Iron the fabric so that it stays in this position.

2. Cut your ribbon in half, creating two 1-yard pieces. Insert one piece in the middle of each side's seam, with about 1 inch of the ribbon hanging out the end and the rest poking inward.

3. Sew a seam down each side, ½ inch from the edge.

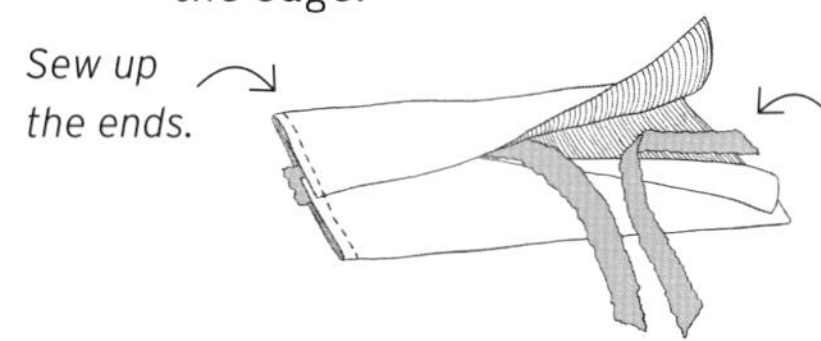

4. Turn the whole thing right-side out. You should have what looks like a long, unstuffed pillow with a ribbon sticking out each end.

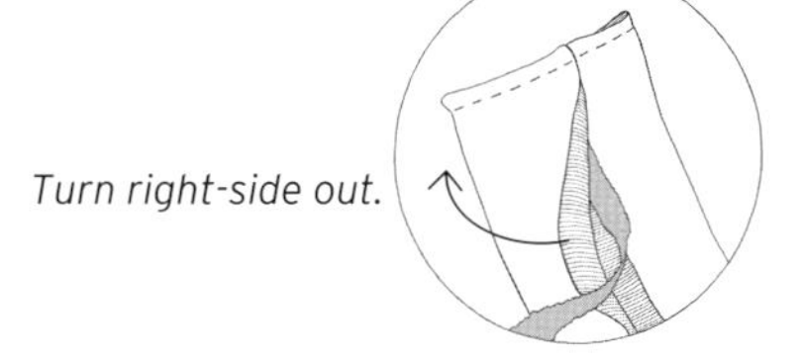

5. To wear, hold the cummerbund against your belly, with the open seam facing in. Wrap the fabric around your middle, crossing the ribbons in the back and bringing them around to the front of the cummerbund. Tie ribbon in a bow to secure.

TOP 10 THINGS TO DO WHILE WEARING Shabby Chic

1. Host a garden affair.
2. Burn groups of white candles in your fireplace.
3. Order some personalized thank-you notes for yourself.
4. Buy a floral slipcover for your couch.
5. Find out more about the history of brocade.
6. Have your initials embroidered on your towels.
7. Learn how to mosaic.
8. Pick up a Mozart CD.
9. Repot your window-box flowers.
10. Crackle-paint an old chandelier antique white.

purses and shoes

WHAT YOU'LL NEED

- Purse with top opening
- Hot glue gun
- 2 yards of black feather trim on a strip of ribbon
- 2 yards of black-and-white feather trim on a strip of ribbon
- Necklace that looks good with purse to use as handle (optional)

Opposite Feathers

This purse was created after I'd brought the original to a friend's wedding. The bride spilled coffee all over the front of my bag, and it was seemingly ruined—making it a perfect candidate for feathering. What I love about this project is that it took less than half an hour and is the perfect, eye-catching accessory for any black, white, or black-and-white outfit.

DIRECTIONS

1. Lay the purse flat on one side. Starting at the bottom, lay a strip of black feather trim across the bag so that the tips of the feathers curve a little bit around the bottom. Hot-glue the ribbon, using enough to seal the sides so the feathers on the edge do not fall out.

2. Get a strip of black-and-white feather trim and glue it across the bag, just above the strip you already attached. Make sure the line is high enough for the row of black feathers to show underneath.

3. Repeat until one side of the purse is covered, alternating strips of black and black-and-white feather trim. Let the glue dry.

4. Flip the purse over and repeat to cover the other side. You'll want to leave the sides uncovered so the purse can still open and close.

5. If the handle matches the feathered design, feel free to leave it. If not, remove the handle. For this purse, I pried open the seam and unstrung the existing pearl handle. I restrung it with beads from an old necklace and then reglued the wire back into the purse in its original groove. You could also just attach the old necklace without the wire and use it as a soft handle.

TOP 10 THINGS TO DO WHILE CARRYING

Opposite Feathers

1 Feather your hair.

2 Strut your stuff.

3 Get binoculars and go bird-watching.

4 Make a feathered hair ornament to match your purse by gluing feathers to the end of a hair stick.

5 Wear a black boa.

6 Hot-glue feathers to a pair of high-heeled sandals for a "boudoir" look.

7 Do the chicken dance.

8 Make eggs over easy.

9 Watch Alfred Hitchcock's movie *The Birds*.

10 Start a Fabergé egg collection.

Variation

Instead of feathers, cover your purse with layers of fringe, lace, or strips of ribbon. Or make a ruffled purse with layers of pleated fabric.

Pansies Purse

Flowers are one of those things that brighten up just about any space. It's almost as if they were made for no other reason than to bring beauty into the world. I like to put real ones in my hair any chance I get. This purse is just a little spot of cheerfulness for any outfit. It's fun, and good for a purse or box in need of a little revamp.

WHAT YOU'LL NEED

- **Old purse with opening at top or hinged box**
- **2 bunches of faux flowers (pansies used here)**
- **Hot glue gun**
- **2 feet of ribbon to match flowers**
- **Scissors**
- **Purse handle (optional)**
- **2 ¼-inch screw-eyes to attach handles (only if you're using a hinged box)**

DIRECTIONS

1. Pluck flowers off a bouquet; they should come off quite easily. If the bottoms of the plastic stems are too long, trim them back, making sure the flowers stay intact.

2. Lay the purse flat on its back. Run a 2-inch line of glue across the top left corner.

3. Place a few flowers next to each other on the glue line. Extend the line of glue, adding more flowers until you've completed one row all the way across. Repeat with another line right below the first line. Prep your flowers so you can glue them on quickly before the glue dries. Continue until the whole front of the purse is covered.

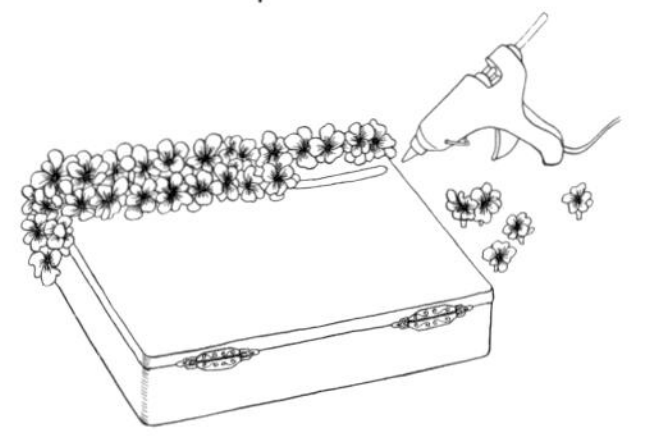

4. Make sure the glue is dry on one side of the purse. Flip over the purse and repeat on the back. Do not put flowers on the sides of the purse if the fabric moves when the purse opens and closes, because the flowers will fall off or the purse might not close properly. You might also want to leave the bottom uncovered so it sits up properly.

5. If you're using an old purse, remove the handle if it does not go with the new look. Attach a new handle by making holes in the top of the purse and running a ribbon loop through each hole; then hook the loops around the handle. Tie a knot on the inside of the purse to secure the handle.

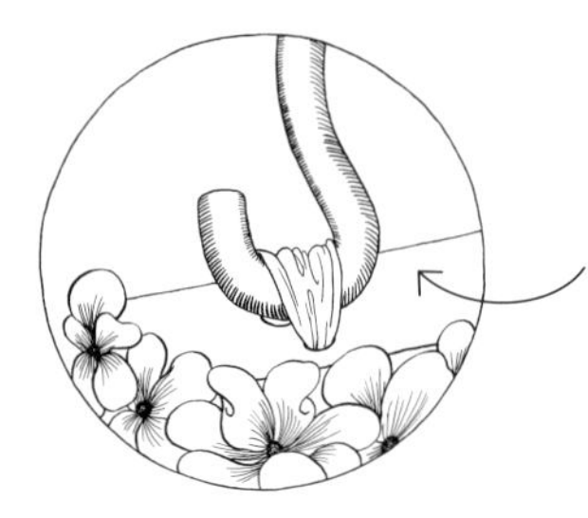

Punch holes in the top and attach a new handle with ribbon.

If your bag has a closure (like the bag I used in the photo, which had a huge magnetic one) and it doesn't match your purses' new look either paint it with acrylic or hot-glue some coordinating fabric to it.

Box Option

If you're using a box that you want to turn into a purse, fasten screw-eyes into the top of the box where the handles meet the box, equidistant from each side. Tie your handle to the eyes with ribbon. If the box doesn't have a closure, you can hot-glue two pieces of ribbon, one to each side, starting about 1 inch on the inside of the purse and extending about 4 inches out of the opening and make a tight bow to close it.

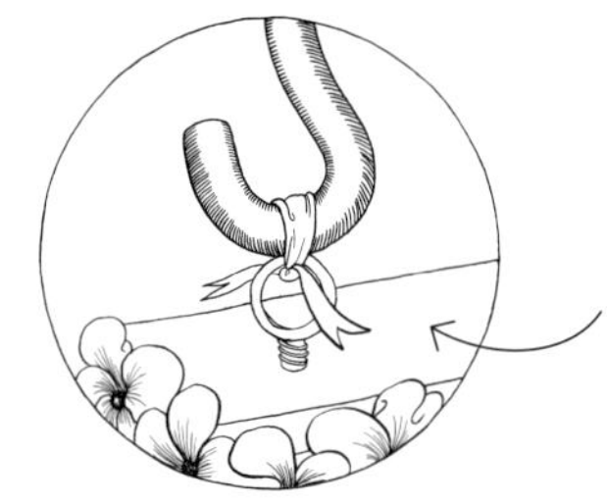

Fasten screw-eyes into box top and then tie handle on with ribbon.

TOP 10 THINGS TO DO WHILE CARRYING YOUR

Pansies Purse

1. Take a flower arranging course.
2. Paint daisies on your bicycle.
3. Wear a big, blooming pink rose in your hair.
4. Create a new fragrance for yourself at the Body Shop.
5. Make pressed bougainvillea cards.
6. Make a salad with edible nasturtiums.
7. Grow a chamomile plant in your garden and start making your own tea.
8. Make a lavender wand.
9. Draw a bath and sprinkle the water with rose petals.
10. Make cupcakes with icing flowers on top.

WHAT YOU'LL NEED

- Piece of plaid silk, 8 × 3 inches
- 1 foot of ribbon
- 2 buttons
- 2 shoe clips
- 2 scraps of felt or leather, each the size of a quarter
- Hot glue gun
- Fray Check
- Needle and thread
- Pinking shears
- Seamstress tape or ruler

General Plaid Regalia

Not to talk your ear off about all the old ladies I used to hang out with when I was a kid, but there was one in particular, Mrs. Copeland, the wife of a retired general who served in World War II. Mrs. Copeland always had dainty shoe clips gracing the toes of her shoes. They were very proper in pearls and rhinestones, swirling shapes, bows, and flowers. Shoe clips make your shoes eye-catching and help your outfit look pulled together. This particular shoe clip also makes me think of a general's medal because of the starlike shape. Officially cute, I must say.

DIRECTIONS

1. Cut eight pieces of silk with your pinking shears, each measuring 1 × 3 inches.

2. Pull some threads out from the ends of each piece to create ragged edges, then apply Fray Check to your ends.

3. Overlap four pieces in a star shape and sew a point in the middle to secure.

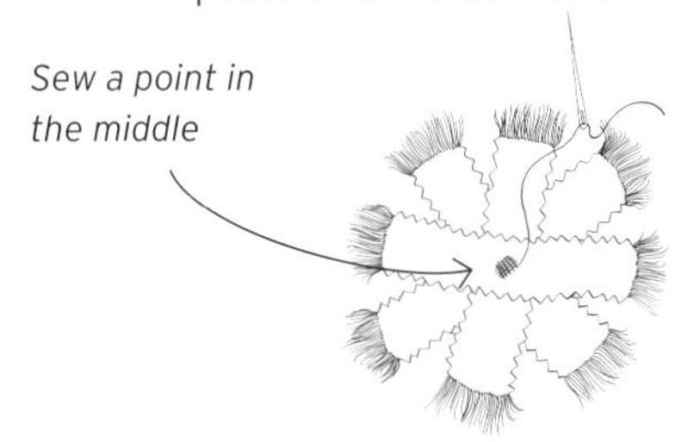

4. Cut the ribbon in half. Take one half and fold it into six loops, then sew to the middle of the silk star.

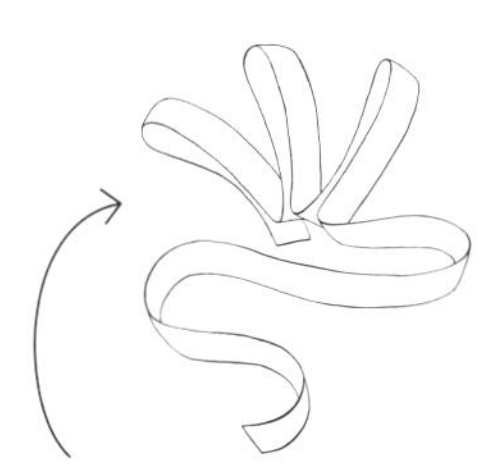

Fold ribbon into six loops.

5. Sew a button to the center to cover all the intersections.

6. Hot-glue everything to a little scrap of felt or leather.

7. Hot-glue the felt or leather to the shoe clip.

8. Repeat steps 3–7 for the other shoe.

TOP 10 THINGS TO DO WHILE WEARING General Plaid Regalia

1 Visit the Motts Military Museum in Groveport, Ohio.

2 Read *Guns, Germs, and Steel*.

3 Look into joining the Daughters of the American Revolution Society.

4 Visit an elderly couple who lived through a war and ask about their experiences.

5 Go see the changing of the guard at Buckingham Palace.

6 Learn to play the French horn.

7 Go horseback riding.

8 Watch *The Patriot*.

9 Find an old army jacket at a military surplus store.

10 Write a letter to a friend in the military who is stationed overseas.

Variation

Make your star with scrap pieces of ribbon instead of silk, and glue an old rock concert pin to the center instead of a button.

WHAT YOU'LL NEED

- 10 pieces of silk ribbon in four different colors, each 1 inch wide × 7 ½ inches long
- 2 oblong pearl-drop beads
- 10 feathers
- 2 shoe clips
- 2 quarter-size pieces of felt
- Hot glue gun
- Needle and thread

Queen Victoria's tea Party toes

There is something regally festive about large puffs of richly hued ribbon. I imagine Queen Victoria wearing these shoes to a royal tea party held in her honor. The hand-dyed ribbons you see here were actually free—they were at a perfume counter for me to mist and take home. Each ribbon color corresponded to a different scent. Of course I tried all of them and ended up with all this pretty ribbon just waiting to be turned into a project. This is a great project for those of you who have small scraps of ribbon lying around.

DIRECTIONS

1. Take four of the silk lengths, one of each color, and place them next to one another, pleating each one in half first. Pinch in the middle and sew together by poking your needle through all the pieces.

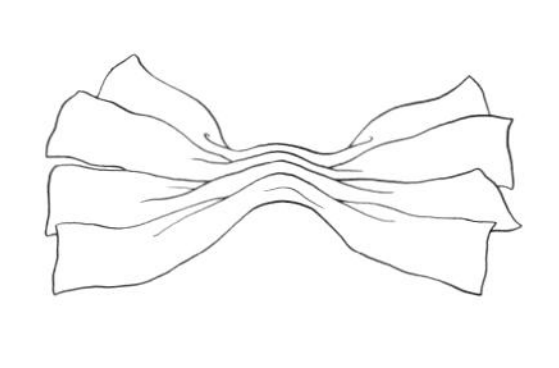

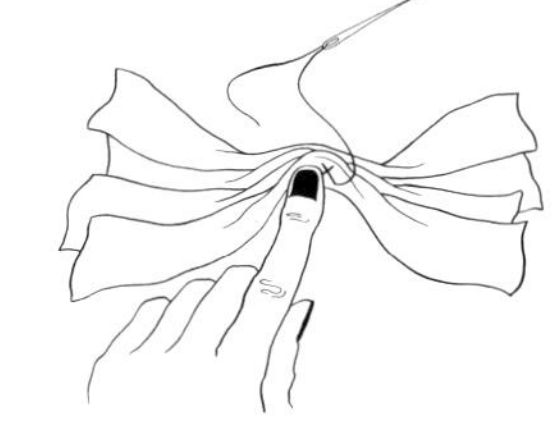

2. Fold over the tips from each side to meet in the middle, and hand-sew to the pinched middle.

Fold tips to meet in the middle.

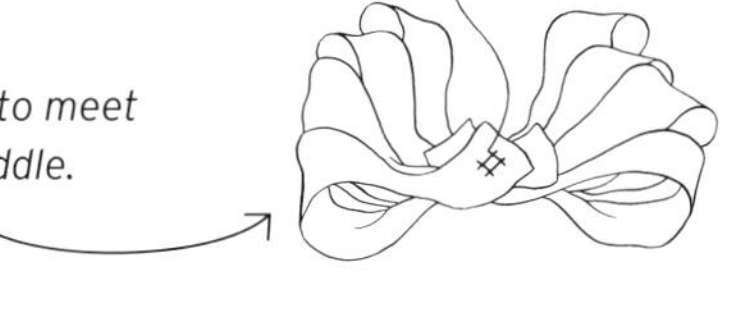

3. Wrap another piece of ribbon around the center a few times, making sure to cover all the raw ends, and sew in back to secure.

4. Sew the end of the pearl bead to the back of the bow.

5. Take your felt piece and hot-glue it to the shoe clip.

6. Hot-glue five feathers to top of felt, then hot-glue the silk bow on top. Clip to your shoe.

7. Repeat steps 1–6 for other shoe clip.

Variation

Hot-glue your ribbon, pearl, and feather creation to a brooch or hair clip for a stylish addition to a jacket or your ponytail.

TOP 10 THINGS TO DO WHILE WEARING

Queen Victoria's Tea Party Toes

1 Visit Windsor Castle.

2 Wear a tiara.

3 Learn to wave like a royal princess.

4 Host a tea party.

5 Figure out whether you have any royal blood; if not, don't feel bad. It doesn't make you any less cool.

6 Watch *The Queen*.

7 Listen to Prince.

8 Wear six strands of pearls.

9 Read a biography of Elizabeth I.

10 Watch *The Princess Diaries.*

Duct-taped and Dangerous

Duct tape is one of those awesome things in life that you can always count on to be strong when you are weak. It is so durable, you never need to worry about it breaking, ripping, or getting wet. I use duct tape to fix everything. The bottom of my car's bumper fell off about a year ago and I duct-taped it up to the front grill. Believe it or not, it's still holding. It is truly miraculous stuff.

WHAT YOU'LL NEED

- **1 roll of silver duct tape, 1½ inches wide**
- **1 roll of pink duct tape, 1½ inches wide**
- **1 roll of yellow duct tape, 1½ inches wide**
- **Scissors**
- **Seamstress tape or ruler**

DIRECTIONS

Make the body

1. Rip 6 pieces of silver duct tape, each 16 inches long. Tape them together horizontally, overlapping each piece ¼ inch. I use the edge of a table to stick on the ends of the tape. This will create a panel of very sticky silver duct tape.

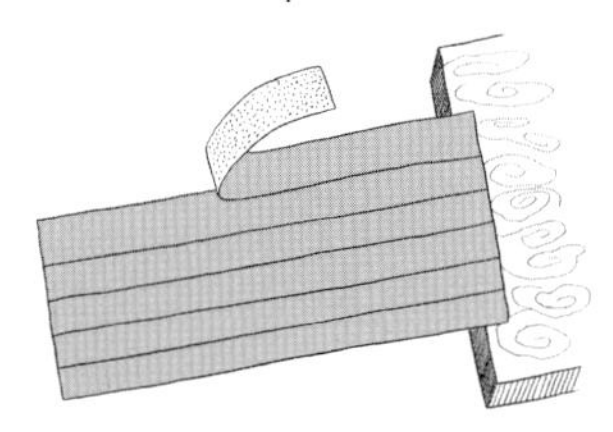

2. Rip 6 pieces of white duct tape, each 16 ½ inches long. Cover the sticky side of your silver "panel" with these strips, using the same overlapping method. Note that the white strips are longer, and ½ inch of them should hang over one side of the silver panel.

3. Bring the two long sides together, forming a tube, with the silver side in the center. Use the excess sticky white tape to tape the "tube" together; then flatten it to form the body of the purse.

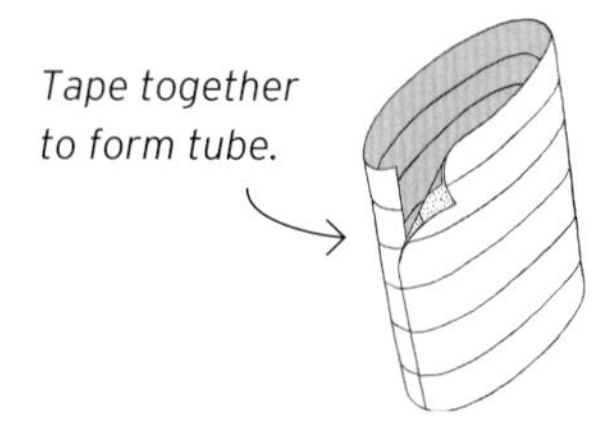

4. Rip two more pieces of white tape, each 9 inches long. Stick them along the purse's seam to reinforce it, folding over the ends into the inside of the purse at top and bottom.

5. Make a ½-inch snip up each side from the bottom, creating two flaps. Fold and overlap the flaps to create a stiff purse bottom. Run a piece of white tape along the bottom and fold up, taping to the sides of the purse. (This might leave a jagged edge, but we'll cover that in a bit.)

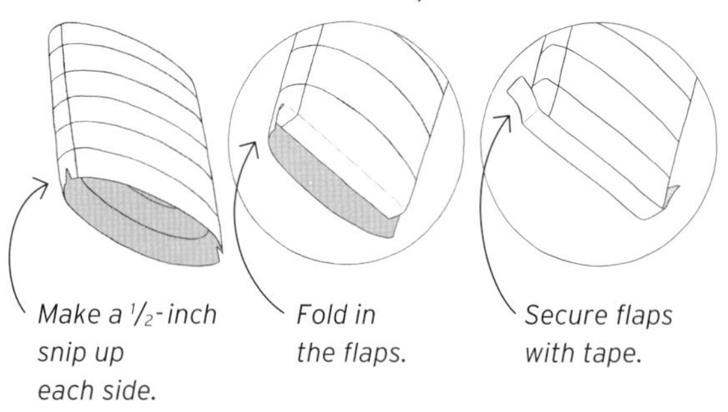

Add the decorations

6. Rip a piece of pink tape 16 inches long. Stick it around the top rim of the purse, folding it over so ⅛ inch shows around the outside.

7. Rip a piece of yellow tape 16 inches long. Run it around the top of the purse, just below the pink rim.

8. Make the ruffle. Tear a piece of pink tape 2 feet long. Fold it in half lenthwise to form a long, narrow strip. Tear off another piece 16 inches long and attach it to the side of a table. Take the folded piece and stick it just beneath the edge of the other piece,

ruffling it as you go so you have a neat, even ruffle attached to a long straight piece of tape. Carefully pull the entire creation from the table and run it around the top of your purse, overlapping the bottom of the yellow strip.

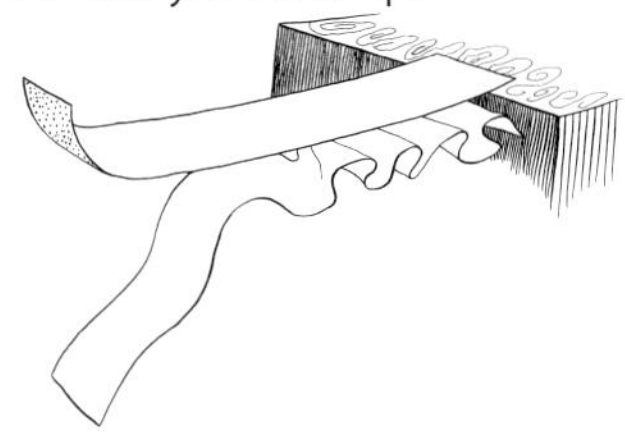

9. Make four yellow triangles and use them to cover the bottom corners of the purse, front and back.

10. Trim any excess white tape sticking out.

Make the straps

11. Rip four pieces of white tape, each 20 inches long. Fold one piece in half lengthwise, then fold a second piece over it to reinforce it. Repeat to make a second strap.

12. Tape both straps to the inside of the purse with silver tape, one on each side, making sure the straps are the same length and distance from the sides.

Variation

For a bigger bag with a longer, thicker handle double the width and length measurements.

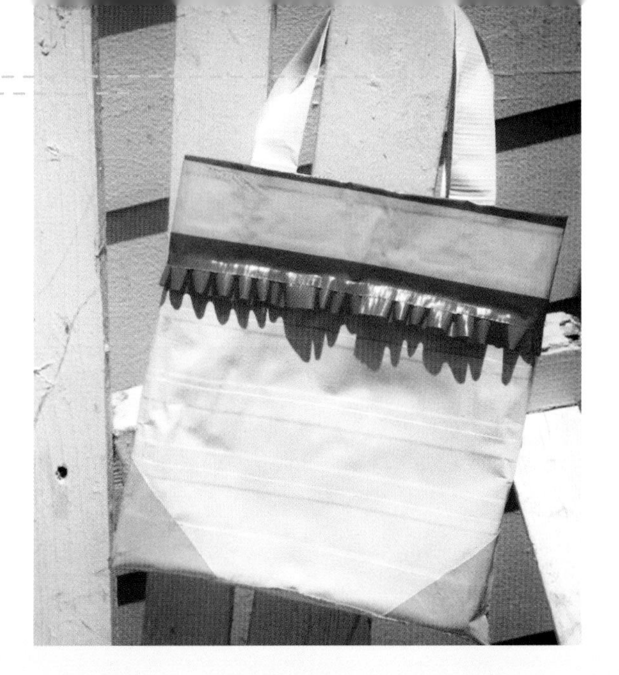

TOP 10 THINGS TO DO WHILE CARRYING

Duct-taped and Dangerous

1 Give it to your pregnant friend to use as a diaper bag.

2 Take it to the gym and stuff it with your sweaty clothes after your workout.

3 Wear it with your yellow rain slicker and jump in a puddle.

4 Rent Gene Kelly's *Singin' in the Rain* and have a sing-along.

5 Pack it up with your wet towel and bikini after a day at the beach.

6 Hose it down when it gets dirty.

7 Watch *The Umbrellas of Cherbourg (Les Parapluies de Cherbourg)*, starring the young Catherine Deneuve, and learn some French.

8 Bring it with you on an exotic vacation to Hawaii.

9 Run through a sprinkler with your bag on your shoulder.

10 Bring it when you go mushroom collecting in the forest.

scarves, ties and a garter!

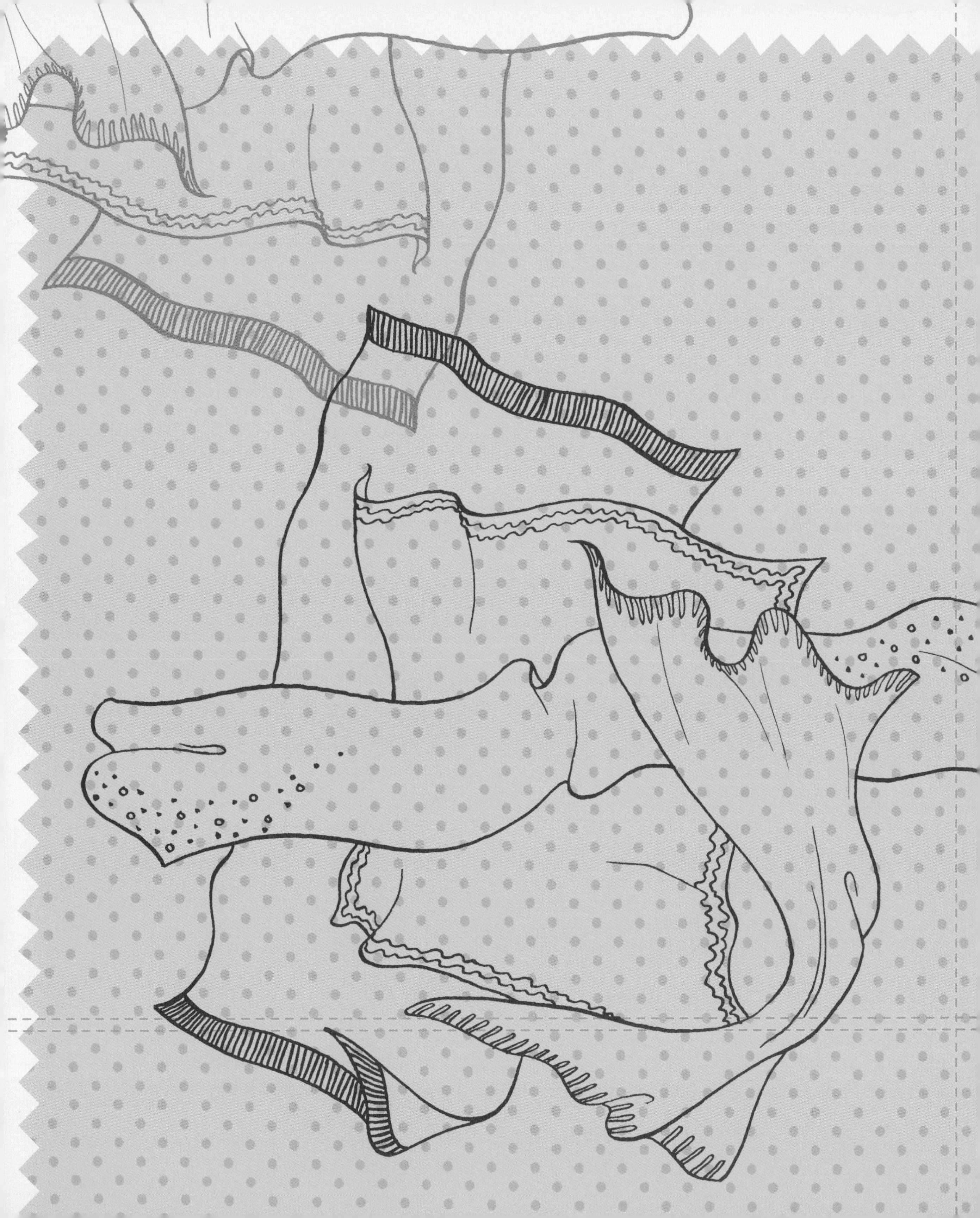

Le St. Tropez

WHAT YOU'LL NEED

- **1 yard of decorative ribbon, ½ inch wide**
- **2–3 yards of wider ribbon, 1½ inches wide**
- **Square silk scarf, 25 × 25 inches**
- **Needle and thread and/or sewing machine**
- **Scissors**
- **Safety pins**
- **Straight pins**

A popular retreat for the stars, St. Tropez is known for its flashy bling style and George Hamilton tans. I've been there only once, but I remember seeing quite a few women with nothing on top but a scarf. I could never figure out how those scarves stayed up, but I guess in the south of France it really doesn't matter either way. This is a safer alternative for the American tourist. Plus, you don't need a million supplies to make this: just a couple yards of ribbon and a scarf and you're ready to jetset.

DIRECTIONS

1. Get the wider, 1½-inch ribbon and find its center point. Mark that point with a safety pin. Wrap the ribbon around your chest, where you want the top of your shirt to lie, and center the safety pin over your cleavage. Use safety pins to mark where each end of the ribbon wraps under your armpits. You should now have three points marked on your ribbon with safety pins.

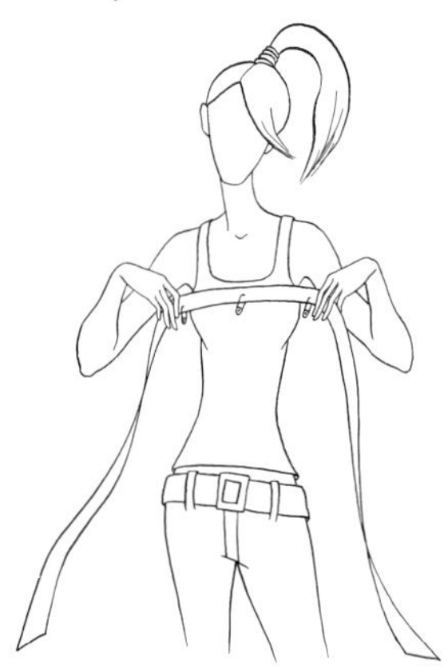

2. Decide which end of the scarf you want to be the top of your shirt. Align the center mark on the ribbon with the center of that scarf edge and pin together, with the ribbon on top and overlapping the scarf's top edge by ¼ inch. Pin the scarf's corners to the two armpit pins. There should be extra scarf material gaping between the pins.

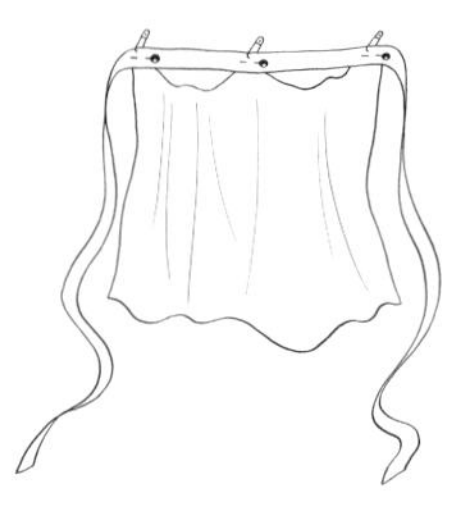

3. You're going to "use up" the extra scarf material by pleating it. Pin the pleats in place evenly along the ribbon.

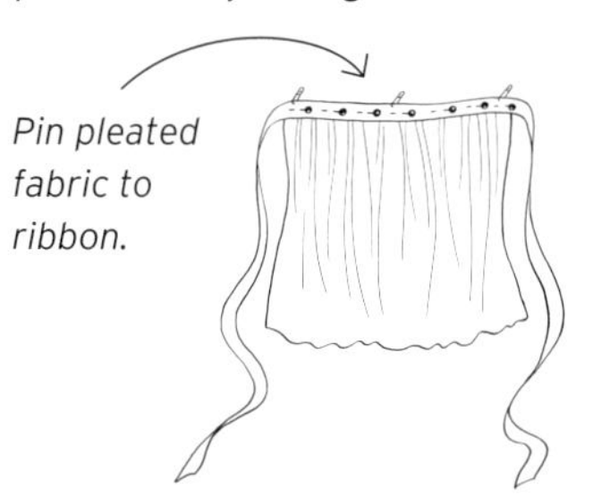

Pin pleated fabric to ribbon.

4. Stitch across, sewing the pleated scarf to the ribbon.

5. Put the top on. Wrap the ribbon over your chest, cross the ends across your back, and bring them around to the front, tying them in a bow as shown. If your ribbon is long enough, you can wrap it twice around your waist.

6. Now add the straps. Mark the points on the top of your shirt where you want each strap to lie. Get the ½-inch ribbon and cut in half. Pin one half to each mark, on the inside. Pull each half across your shoulder to the back and pin to the top of the ribbon there (you may need a friend to help with this).

Pin straps in place.

7. Take the shirt off. Hand-sew each strap in place with a point stitch.

Variation

For a raw look, use soft leather or Ultrasuede instead of ribbon.

TOP 10 THINGS TO DO WHILE WEARING

Le St. tropez

1. Go to the Cannes Film Festival.
2. Draw on your eyeliner like Brigitte Bardot.
3. Ride on a yacht with a millionaire.
4. Eat oysters and drink champagne.
5. Treat yourself to a spa.
6. Go to a casino.
7. Ride in a private jet.
8. Wear red lipstick.
9. Watch the James Bond film *For Your Eyes Only*.
10. Eat crême brulée with a silver spoon.

WHAT YOU'LL NEED

- Choker necklace, about 18 inches long
- Square silk scarf, 25 × 25 inches
- 2 yards of ribbon, 1 inch wide
- Needle and thread
- Scissors
- Straight pins

Copacabana

When I imagine an Amazon goddess, I see Danielle in this hot number. This bold, colorful top is really simple to make and won't take you more than half an hour if you've got all the stuff. It's a great beach shirt, concert getup, or party top. Just make sure the necklace you use secures tightly—if it comes apart, you'll end up flashing not only your date, but everyone else, too.

TOP 10 THINGS TO DO IN Copacabana

1. Drink a Caipirinha.
2. Learn to samba.
3. Listen to João Gilberto.
4. Bronze yourself.
5. Celebrate Carnivale in Brazil.
6. Learn Portuguese.
7. Watch *That Man from Rio* starring Jean-Paul Belmondo.
8. Buy a Brazilian bikini.
9. Fry some bananas.
10. Learn to do capoeira.

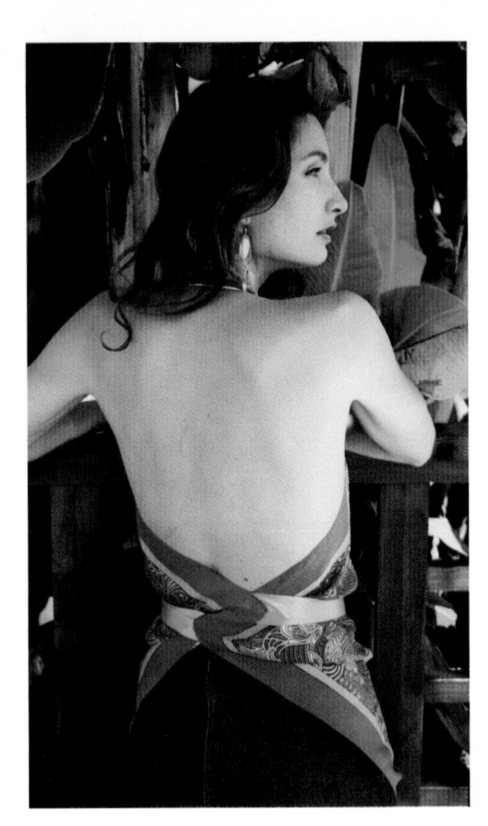

DIRECTIONS

1. Fold one corner of the scarf 5 inches over the necklace and pin. Sew in place with a tight straight stitch running along the line of the necklace, leaving ¼ inch of space so that the scarf can pleat and bunch around the necklace when worn.

2. Cut the ribbon in half. Sew one length of ribbon to each side corner of the scarf, hiding the stitching on the back.

3. To wear, close the choker around your neck, then wrap the two ribbons around your back at your waist and tie in front.

WHAT YOU'LL NEED

- Black garter
- Lace V-neck collar; or a piece of lace, 2 feet wide x 1 foot long, and a doily
- 1 button, 2 inches diameter
- 5 inches of black ribbon for button loop
- Needle and thread (sewing machine optional)
- Straight pins

Bachelorette Forever

Garters are one of those things that everyone seems to have but no one seems to wear more than once. The garter used for this project is the one my girlfriends made me wear during my bachelorette party. Here, I've turned it into a sexy little halter and paired it with a strapless black dress, making it a bit dressier for an evening out.

DIRECTIONS

1. If you're making your own lace collar, trim the piece of lace so that the top is 2 feet wide and the bottom is in a scalloped, collar shape. If you like, use a doily as a pattern.

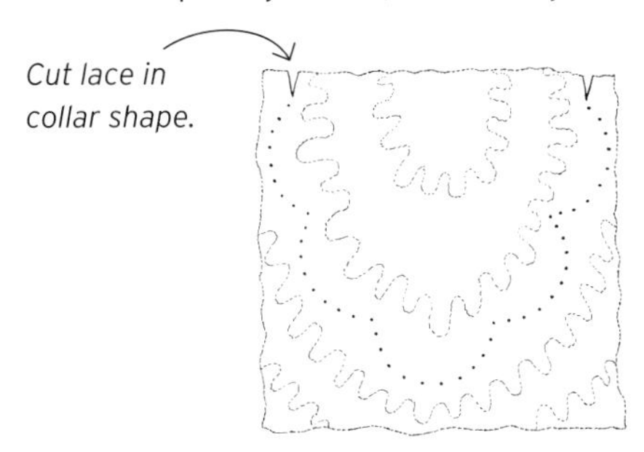

2. Open the side seam of the garter carefully. Pin one end of the garter to an immovable object, like the arm of your couch.

3. Stretch the garter to its full length. Take the top edge of your lace piece and pin one end to each end of the garter, on the garter's back side. Then pin the rest of the lace along the garter.

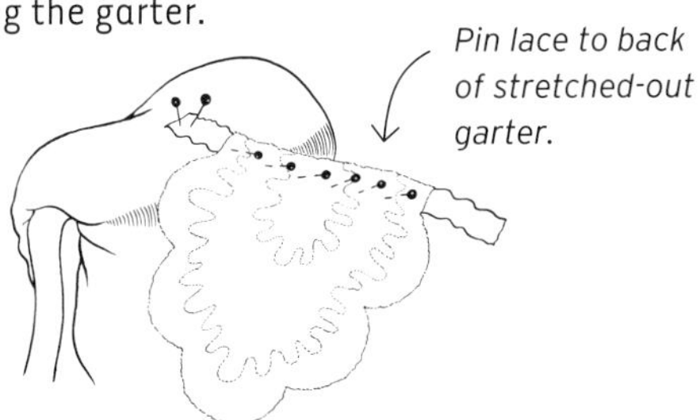

4. Zigzag stitch or hand-sew the pinned lace to the garter. Trim off any excess lace sticking out the top.

5. Sew a button to one end of the garter. Sew a ribbon loop to the other end that's big enough to loop around the button for closure.

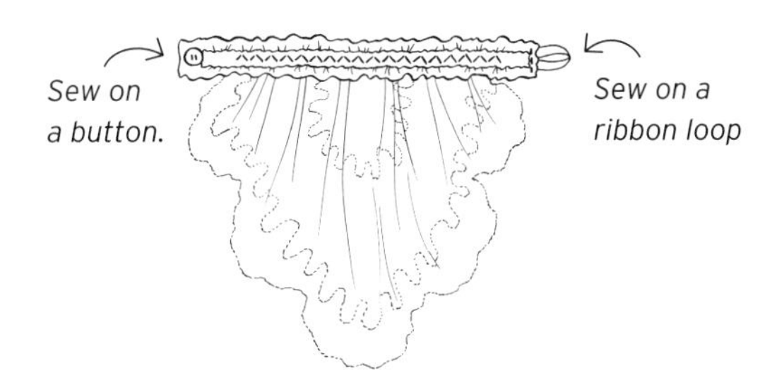

Variation

Make a plain black dress match your lace collar by adding a 3-inch-wide ruffle to the bottom of your dress. Just pleat a piece of lace along the hem of your dress and sew along the inside with a straight stitch.

TOP 10 THINGS TO DO WHILE WEARING

Bachelorette Forever

1. Drink a Cosmopolitan.
2. Spend a weekend in Manhattan with your best girlfriends.
3. Google an old boyfriend.
4. Wear stilettos.
5. Paint your nails candy-apple red.
6. Dance until dawn, then go straight to brunch.
7. Give all the men in your life nicknames.
8. Watch reruns of *Sex and the City*.
9. Send your best friend flowers, just because she's great.
10. Ask out a cute guy or two.

Swing Around the Posy

Some days, it's just nice to wear something loose for a day of fun in the sun. You can run around in the grass and play tag football, laze around making daisy-chains, and eat as much as you want without people wondering if you're preggers. I'm imagining a plateful of juicy barbecued ribs, potato salad, and grilled corn dripping with butter. The silk shift doubles as a napkin for those messy meals as well.

WHAT YOU'LL NEED

- **Cross-your-heart stretch shirt in an acrylic, polyester, Lycra, or cotton blend (can be long-sleeved, short-sleeved, or tank top)**
- **Piece of lace, 45 × 2 inches**
- **Scarf made of polyester, satin, or silk, 16 × 45 inches.**
- **3 feet of ribbon, 1 inch wide**
- **Needle and thread and/or sewing machine**
- **Scissors**
- **Fabric pencil**
- **Straight pins**

DIRECTIONS

1. Fold the scarf in half and mark where the middle is.

2. Fold the shirt in half and mark where the center of the shirt is at the bottom of the bustline.

3. Pin the middle of the scarf to the middle of the shirt, with the scarf on top, its top edge aligned with the bustline.

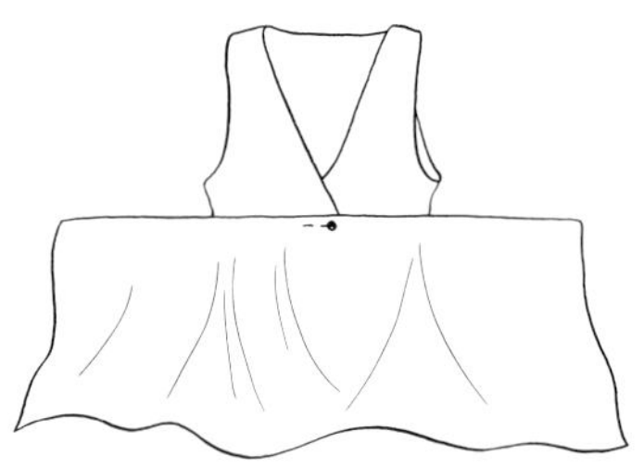

4. Starting at the midpoint, pin the scarf to the shirt along the bustline on one side, arranging the scarf in tiny pleats as you go. End at the side seam. I had 6 inches of extra scarf left over on that side; leave this portion hanging free.

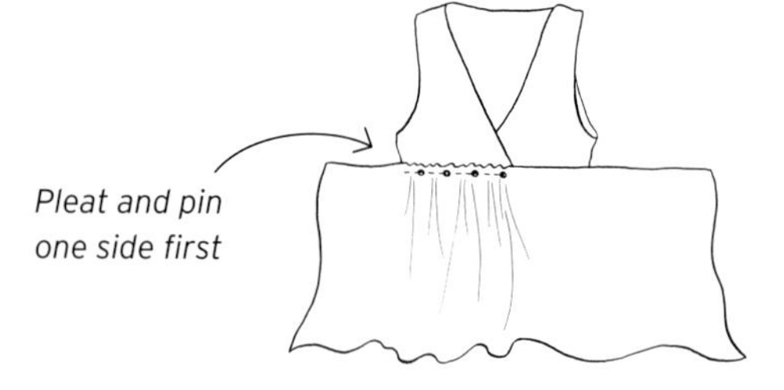

5. Mark 6 inches (or whatever you measured as extra on the first side) from the other end of the scarf and pin that point to the other side seam of the shirt. Starting back at the midpoint, pin down the second side of the scarf, repeating the pleating and ending at the second side seam.

6. Sew the pleated seam to the shirt, ending at both side seams.

7. Sew the lace along the top of the scarf, to cover the bumpy seam. Sew the lace all the way to both ends of the scarf.

8. Cut the ribbon in half. Sew each piece to one top corner of the scarf, on the inside.

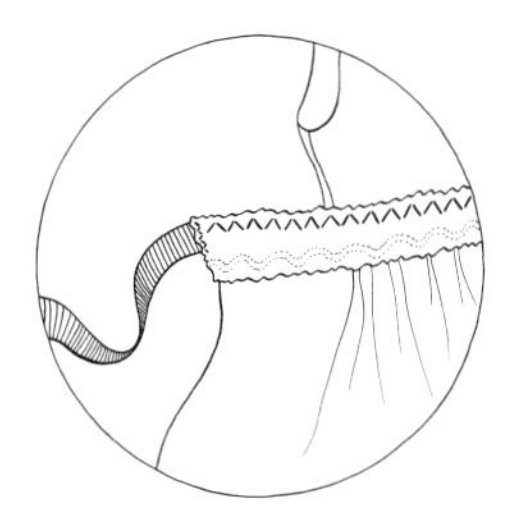

9. To wear, put the shirt on, then wrap the extra scarf ends around your back. Tie as shown.

Optional pockets

If the shirt was long-sleeved and you cut the sleeves off, you may want to use some of that extra fabric to add pockets to your shirt.

1. Split the arm fabric at the seams and lay it flat.
2. Draw two hearts on the fabric. Cut them out.
3. Pin the hearts to the scarf in symmetrical locations and sew around the edges. Add ribbons if desired.

TOP 10 THINGS TO DO WHILE WEARING Swing Around the Posy

1. Go on a picnic with friends.
2. Make a key lime pie.
3. Go barefoot.
4. Play hopscotch.
5. Run through a field of sunflowers.
6. Listen to the Dixie Chicks.
7. Stargaze on a hot summer night.
8. Make a daisy-chain bracelet.
9. Run through a sprinkler.
10. Hug a tree.

Variation

Layer a few sheer scarves for a summery feel.

Daddy's Girl

WHAT YOU'LL NEED

- 15–20 neckties
- Pair of short shorts with zipper fly
- 2 small snaps
- Needle and thread
- Sewing machine
- Straight pins
- Seamstress tape or ruler

I love that my dad actually wore all these crazy ties at some point in his life. If you look closely, you'll see how bold they are in design and color: bright turquoise, pinks, and oranges; wide and narrow. Now he goes for a really neutral palette, but I love how once upon a time he had a really daring sense of color and style.

DIRECTIONS

1. Measure 18 inches from the bottom of each tie (the skinny end) and cut across. The long skinny ends will be left over. Do not worry about these; we will use them a bit later.

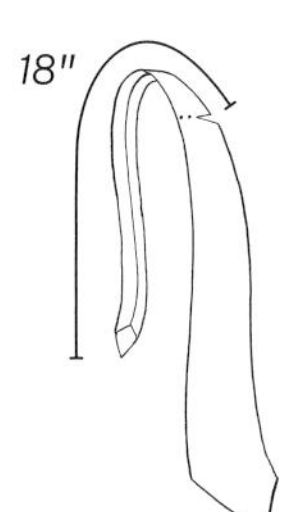

2. Take your shorts and pin your first tie just to the right of the zipper fly, leaving 2 inches of the tie hanging over the waistband. Using a straight stitch, sew 4 inches down the *left* edge of the tie, starting at the waistband. The remaining 12 inches will flop loosely.

3. Pin a second tie just to the right of the first tie, at the exact same length. They should butt right up next to each other. You're going to sew down the *right* side of the first tie and the *left* side of the second tie at the same time. Use a zigzag stitch on the widest setting so that the thread hits both ties. Again, sew down only 4 inches.

4. Repeat step 3 until the whole circumference of the shorts is covered in side-by-side ties—stop when you are 1 inch from the fly. Make sure the shorts stay pulled tight throughout, so that they don't pucker.

5. When you add the last tie before the fly, leave its right side loose. Get one more tie and pin its left edge to the loose right side of the previous tie. Use a zigzag stitch to sew the two ties together *but not to the shorts*, so that they form a loose flap that covers the fly. Sew one big snap to the top corner of the tie flap. Close the flap and mark where the snap falls on the other side of the skirt. Sew the bottom part of the snap here.

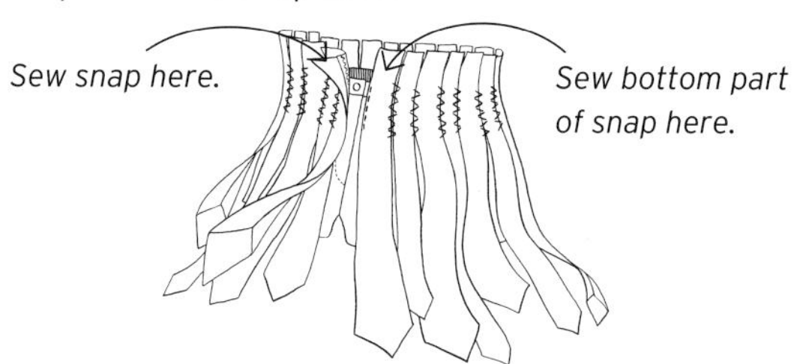

6. Take the top of the neckties and fold them over the waistband, making a nice clean edge. Using a whipstitch, sew them down from the inside, making sure the stitching doesn't show through on the outside. For the ties that form the flap, fold over the raw edges and use a whipstitch to sew them on the back of the ties (this will allow the flap to open and close).

7. Try on your creation. You will see holes here and there where the ties do not cover your legs. Take the long skinny ends of the ties and pin them to the shorts underneath, to cover the holes. Take off the skirt and zigzag stitch the top raw edges of these pieces to the shorts. Try it on again to check for more holes.

8. Voilà! Spin around in your new skirt and watch the ties fly!

TOP 10 THINGS TO DO IN YOUR

Daddy's Girl Skirt

1. Call your dad and ask him for more ties.
2. Pamper yourself like a little girl.
3. Ask people who you look more like: your mom, dad, or neither.
4. Start a family tree.
5. Look into visiting the town where your dad was born.
6. Ask Dad to reinstate your allowance.
7. Organize a family picnic.
8. Give your dad yet another necktie.
9. Learn how to tie a necktie.
10. Surprise your dad with his favorite meal.

Acknowledgments

Thank you to everyone who made this book possible: Carrie Grim's great eye for catching the "moment" not a second too late; Dany Paragouteva, a true artiste whose illustrations made the book beautiful; Kate Couture (www.couturefaces.com), the talented and ever-so-patient makeup artist, for accommodating my eyebrow requests and making us pretty!; Danielle, who never takes a bad picture and is even lovelier than she is beautiful (you're always in my Top Ten!); Gina, the hipper-than-anyone-I've-met stylist who doubled as a hot model, Toyin, Amanda, and Harley for taking precious time out of their day to model. A big thanks to everyone at Watson-Guptill—Julie Mazur for believing that I could write a book; Cathy Hennessy, for making my words make sense; Julie Duquet for the beautiful art direction; woolypear, for the awesome design; Alyn Evans, for managing the production; and Andrea Glickson for getting the word out.

Thanks to my friends and family who have given me so much support through all my "great" ideas and the messes that accompany them: Mom, Dad, Ben, you are always there for me; Cindy the #1 mama, Lizzie, Tina C, Lady K Unicorn, Phoebe, Jeni, Camille, Monterey FBC, the crew at Anderson, Lauren Powell, Jonathan Fong, Gail, Leeta, Joella, Gareth, Rene and Sara, Scott, Chris Miller, Tina I., Jacquie Jordan, the Petersons, the Beales, and the Kinsellas. Special thanks to Kathleen—who lets me foray into crafty-land.

The most specialest of thanks to my #1 Chankle Christopa for singing me to sleep every night and for loving me unconditionally. And Olaf the Grey . . .

Resource Guide

Most of the supplies used to make the projects in this book are readily available no matter where you are—at your local craft store or online. Wedding gown seamstresses might know good local resources for lace, and hand-crocheted collars. Old lingerie is also a great resource for all the lace projects in the book. Avoid for vintage fabrics that may be past their prime and starting to decompose; all natural fabrics have a shelf life. Feathers on strips might be difficult to find locally but are available online.

LACE AND RIBBON

The lace trim and ribbon for Frilled and Fabulous, Laced with Charm, Ruffled Around the Edges, Naughty See's Candy Lady, Swing Around the Posy, and Mademoiselle Coco all came from:
Button and Trim Expo
828 Maple Ave.
Los Angeles, CA 90014-2204
(213) 622-2323

Lace fabric by the yard:
Michael Levine Inc.
919 Maple Ave.
Los Angeles, CA 90015-1811
(213) 622-6259

Online sources for lace:
www.**eBay**.com
www.**cheeptrims**.com
www.**fashionfabricsclub**.com
www.**trimfabric**.com
www.**buttons4u**.com

Ribbon for Turtleneck Purse:
F&S Fabrics for the Home
10624 W. Pico Blvd.
Los Angeles, CA 90064
(310) 441-2477

Ribbon for Highland Lass and Shabby Chic Belt:
www.**Michaels**.com

FEATHERS

Feather trim for Opposite Feathers:
Maple Craft
925 Maple Ave.
Los Angeles, CA 90015
(213) 622-9602

BUTTONS

M&J Trimming
1008 Avenue of the Americas
New York, NY 10018
(212) 391-9072
www.mjtrim.com

SCARVES

The Rosebowl Flea Market
(second Sunday of every month)
1001 Rose Bowl Drive
Pasadena, CA 91103
(323) 560-SHOW (7469)

FLOWERS

The flowers for Pansies Purse are from:
Jo-Ann Fabrics
(check site for a store near you)
www.joann.com
Silk Flowers Express
www.silkflowersexpress.com

SHOE CLIPS

BJ's Craft Supplies
www.bjcraftsupplies.com

PURSE HANDLES

www.**eBay**.com

CLOTHING

Salvation Army and Goodwill Industries thrift stores can be great resources. To find a shop in your area, check:
www.**goodwill**.org
www.**salvationarmyusa**.org

Shop online at:
www.**shopgoodwill**.com

MISCELLANEOUS

Grommets:
www.**seattlefabrics**.com

INDEX